College Style Sheet

Fourth Canadian Edition

Jon Furberg
&
Richard Hopkins
English Department
Langara College
Vancouver, BC

49TH AVENUE PRESS
LANGARA COLLEGE, VANCOUVER, BRITISH COLUMBIA, CANADA

Jon Furberg
1944-1992

49th AVENUE PRESS
Langara College, 100 West 49th Avenue, Vancouver, BC, Canada   V5Y 2Z6

Distributor:
BENDALL BOOKS
P.O. Box 115, Mill Bay, BC   V0R 2P0
ELECTRONIC MAIL: bendallbooks@islandnet.com
WORLD WIDE WEB: http://www.islandnet.com/bendallbooks

COLLEGE STYLE SHEET
Fourth Canadian Edition

Material from *A Casebook of Ideologies* by Macdonald Burbidge © 1990 reprinted with permission of 49th Avenue Press. Sample essay pages reproduced with permission of Leslie Peeler, Jeff Webster, and Tim Hopkins.

Printed in Canada
99 98 97 96   4 3 2

CANADIAN CATALOGUING IN PUBLICATION DATA
Furberg, Jon, 1944-1992.
  College style sheet

  Includes index.
  ISBN 1-896661-00-9
    1. Report writing. 2. English language—Rhetoric
I. Hopkins, Richard, 1936-   II. Title.
PE1408.F87 1996   808'.02   C96-910311-5

Contents

Preface & Acknowledgments v

Introduction 1

Standards of Style 2

Types of Essays 4

Parts of Essays 9

Presentation of Essays 16

Word Processing Tips 20

Handling Mechanical Details 22

Avoiding Discriminatory Language 24

Avoiding Plagiarism 24

Quoting Effectively 29

Acknowledging Sources 42

Works Cited 52

Sample Citations 56
    Print Sources 56
    Government Sources 65
    Nonprint Sources 68

The APA Style of Documentation 74
    Documenting Research in Sociology 79
    Documenting Research in Biology 79

The Note Style of Documentation 81

Index 89

Sample Pages
Title Page (MLA style) 9
Alternative Title Page 11
Text Page (MLA style) 18
Works Cited Page (MLA style) 54
Text Page (APA style) 75
References (APA style) 78
Text and Notes (Note style) 83

Preface & Acknowledgments

The *College Style Sheet* is guided in general by the standards of documentation presented by Joseph Gibaldi in the fourth edition of the *MLA Handbook for Writers of Research Papers*, although it also includes guidelines contained in other pertinent texts (listed under "Standards of Style," pages 2-3). This edition of the *College Style Sheet* incorporates the *MLA Handbook's* most recent changes and additions. These include guidelines for the documentation of electronic sources with examples, and a (welcome) change to the spacing of items in works cited entries. Also found in this edition are other detailed changes and refinements scattered throughout the text, plus a new section that expands on the rather brief comments previously offered on the use of word processors.

The *Style Sheet* recognizes that research essay conventions may not always suit all types of essays or the preferences of all instructors. Alternatives to MLA style are therefore offered in some cases, usually accompanied by the recommendation that students consult their instructors about which style to follow. In this way, the *Style Sheet* admits, within limits, some of the style variations that may still be preferred in some academic departments. For consistency's sake, MLA style is given precedence, but students can easily look beyond it to find the suggested alternatives.

* * *

Langara Style Sheet was the heading on a folded, single-sheet documentation guide composed in 1974 by Alan Dawe, of the English department at the then Langara campus of Vancouver Community College. From this bare-bones beginning, it developed into a pamphlet, inspired by suggestions from students and faculty as they used the sheet in a variety of courses and disciplines. By 1983, it was widely used in colleges in British Columbia, and the name *College Style Sheet* was adopted. In the mid 1980s, departments other than English were offering descriptions of the documentation styles of their respective disciplines; major changes were announced by the most influential arbiter of style, the Modern Language Association of America (MLA); moreover, several important aspects of style, such as the use of quotations and references, deserved more attention—all these were addressed in the 1988 edition. In 1993 the first US edition appeared, incorporating futher changes and revisions. Throughout this process, we tried to maintain the spirit of brevity and simplicity of the original style sheet.

I thank most heartily those colleagues and students at Langara College who made helpful suggestions and contributions that they might find incorporated here, more or less intact. I also thank publisher Raymond Bendall for his indispensible assistance and for his patience and encouragement, too.

Most particularly I am indebted to Jon Furberg, my colleague and friend, whose passing still seems unbelievable. A lover of life and literature, Jon was a remarkable teacher, and his contribution to this work simply cannot be calculated. The *College Style Sheet* stands as a testament to his dedication to his teaching, and to his students.

Richard Hopkins
April 1996

Introduction

The *College Style Sheet* is not a composition text or a handbook of grammar, punctuation, and usage; it is a guide to help you present essays—especially research essays—according to current conventions of physical layout and documentation of sources. All assignments requiring a paper in which you make use of someone else's words, ideas, or data also require that you acknowledge both your sources and your specific use of them.

Each discipline, or field of study, follows a particular system, or "style," for presenting research material and for directing the reader to the original location of this information. Careful study and imitation of the appropriate conventions outlined here will save you hours of trial and error, and should result in improved grades.

This style guide incorporates, with a few modifications, the most current (1995) revision of the documentation system described by the Modern Language Association of America (MLA) which advocates *text references* and a list of *works cited* for the acknowledgment of sources in essay writing. The MLA system is standard for English and other humanities courses.

Some frequently used terms need clarification. The word *style* signifies the way source material is presented and documented; it does not refer to the quality of your expression. By style is meant the accepted conventions regarding the form and placement of quotations, references to sources (whether summarized, paraphrased, or quoted), works cited pages (bibliographies), page layout and numbering, title pages, and the like.

The word *text* means the body of your essay (your sentences) including quotations and parenthetical references. A *reference* is the specific acknowledgment of your use of an external source of information; it may appear directly in your sentence or indirectly in a parenthesis, footnote, or endnote. The purpose of a reference is to direct the reader to a corresponding citation.

A *citation* is the full, formal statement of the publishing details for each source. Citations appear in alphabetical order in a list called "Works Cited" at the end of the essay.

This guide also describes the note style (often required for History papers) and the American Psychological Association, or APA, style required for Psychology papers. Variants of APA style are used for other social sciences (e.g., Sociology) and some physical sciences (e.g., Biology)—these are also discussed here. Remember that when your essay makes any use of secondary material, you are "doing research," and conventions govern the way you should acknowledge it. Ask each of your instructors which pages of the *Style Sheet* are pertinent to his or her assignments. Some may not express a preference for one style over another; nevertheless, you must choose one and be consistent. Do not attempt to invent your own. Treat your essay as though you were offering it for publication.

Standards of Style

Academic disciplines rely upon certain standard manuals for models that demonstrate the accepted form of quotations, references, and source citations.

English

After 1984, English faculties began to abandon footnotes and bibliography in favour of the parenthetical references and list of works cited recommended by the MLA. The *College Style Sheet* summarizes the main features of this style. For a full discussion, consult:

Gibaldi, Joseph. MLA Handbook for Writers of Research Papers. 4th ed. New York: MLA, 1995.

This work should be available for quick consultation at the reference desk of your campus library, on short-term loan at the reserve desk, or for sale in the campus bookstore.

Psychology

Psychology papers employ a system of parenthetical references that stress author and date. The style authority is:

American Psychological Association. Publication Manual of the American Psychological Association. 4th ed. Washington, DC: APA, 1994.

The rudiments of APA style are presented in this *Sheet* (see pages 74-78) together with a sample page and list of works cited. For further information, consult the full *Manual*.

Sociology and Biology

Both disciplines use variations of basic APA style that are illustrated here (see pages 79-80) with examples and notes on distinguishing features.

History and Political Science

These disciplines have tended to retain the traditional footnote style, with some modern variations. The MLA offers its own version of conventions for note style, but for many academics the basic text is still "Turabian":

Turabian, Kate L. A Manual for Writers of Term Papers, Theses, and Dissertations. 5th ed. Chicago: U of Chicago P, 1987.

This text should be available at the library reference desk and in the campus bookstore. The note style is discussed on pages 81-87 of this *Sheet*.

Types of Essays

Before beginning a writing assignment, determine what *type* of essay you are expected to produce. Make sure you know the desired length and scope of the essay, and stick to the limits imposed by your instructor. Does the essay require quotations and references? Should it merely report existing information and ideas? Or are you to offer a *thesis* of your own—the key idea you present to the reader and support by using examples, logically developed arguments, and often research material as well?

Except where noted below, avoid the first-person pronoun, "I," in your essays. Any sentence can be rewritten to remove the self-conscious "I," "me," "my," "mine." It is not necessary to write, "In my opinion," "I believe," "I feel," etc., since the reader assumes your authorship. Similarly, it is redundant, and dull, to begin an essay with a statement of intention such as, "In the following essay, I shall try to prove. . . . "

Personal Experience Essay

In some courses, you may be asked to narrate an event in your life that illustrates a significant truth you have discovered. In this case, write from a first-person point of view (using "I," "me," etc.), and employ vivid sensory language to help draw your reader into the scene. Dialogue is often a valuable means of dramatizing your story; if you use dialogue, imitate the conventions of paragraphing, punctuation, and quotation employed in published short stories or novels.

Expository Essay

A common assignment in many introductory English courses is a short expository essay (about five paragraphs, 350-600 words) in which you either offer information or explain your point of view on a topic you already know about.

These two general kinds of exposition vary according to your intention. One mainly gives information ("Why People Pray"); the other mainly defends an opinion ("Why Prayer Should [or Should

Not] Be Permitted in Public Schools"). Here, the intent of each essay is obvious from its title (they could easily be combined to form a longer essay).

Typically, the short expository essay begins with a paragraph that announces the *topic* (subject matter) and builds to a *thesis statement* in which you state your point of view. Then follows the middle portion of your text, consisting of three or more paragraphs of supporting evidence and reasoned discussion based *mainly* on your personal knowledge, experience, and judgment (but not necessarily excluding material from secondary sources). The essay ends with a paragraph that restates the thesis more emphatically and possibly suggests wider implications. A good ending does not merely summarize.

Research Essay

Unlike the expository essay, a research essay *must* present information and ideas gathered from a variety of sources outside your own experience and knowledge. You must consult and use other people's work. In some sense, all learning is the product of research: our understanding of the world develops and changes as we talk with others, read newspapers, magazines, and books, watch films and television, and observe and react to events around us. When we want to know the answer to an important question, we often find we have to seek help in a source outside ourselves.

In a formal research essay, you must offer a well-developed thesis supported by convincing evidence and opinion found in appropriate sources that are referred to in your text and given credit with full citations in a list of works cited placed at the end of the essay.

Basically, there are two kinds of research. "Primary research" generates new or up-to-date information from interviews, experiments, surveys, or other direct observations. When you are asked to view a painting or read a short story or poem, and then to give your ideas or interpretation, you are also doing primary research—the particular work directly before you provides the sole source of evidence upon which your judgment depends.

"Secondary research" relies upon already published information and ideas found mainly in libraries—in books, scholarly

5

journals, magazines, audiotapes, videotapes, CD-ROMs, micro-forms, and so on—but also, increasingly, on the Internet. Al-though many assignments require secondary research alone, some combine the two kinds.

Through research you enlarge your knowledge and under-standing of a subject and thus your capacity to draw intelligent, forceful conclusions. Some assignments ask only that you prove you have understood a problem; others, that you commit yourself to a solution.

Research essays regularly employ quotation (also paraphrase and summary), text references (or notes), and a list of works cited. Sometimes other aids such as graphs, tables, and diagrams are helpful. Your research, from a *variety* of reliable sources (one or two are insufficient), must be incorporated logically as the essay develops. The key is to keep your thesis in mind always. What are you trying to prove? What are you trying to illustrate?

Try to find sources that are authoritative whenever you do research (particularly when using the Internet)—some instructors will turn to your list of works cited, to see how current and full your research has been, even before they read your text.

Literary Insight Essay

English courses in short fiction, poetry, drama, film, and the novel require papers in which you interpret, and perhaps evalu-ate, a work of literary or cinematic art. There are several ways you can read and meaningfully discuss a work of literature or any other art form: (1) as a created thing, interesting in itself; (2) as a mirror of significant truths about the external world; (3) as a stimulus that calls forth inner feelings and self-awareness; and (4) as the expression of an artist with unique skills, intelligence, and character.

Your instructor may ask only for a personal interpretation of the work at hand. In this case, you are doing primary research; the essay offers your own "insight" without reference to published criticism. You should summarize, paraphrase, and quote the liter-ary text with sufficient frequency to illustrate the key points of your analysis. In-class essay tests are of this kind, as are some home papers. Remember that *your insight is your thesis*.

Term papers, however, usually require that you do secondary research—finding agreement, controversy, and radically different approaches to the same work, or author, to provide support for your own point of view. By consulting, citing, and quoting pertinent critical works in the library, you give the essay greater authority.

Technical Essay

Science courses sometimes require essays in which you record observations, experiments, data, etc., to illustrate your understanding of a particular scientific principle. You may have to describe a procedure, explain a law, or define a certain term.

Research Report

Research reports and research essays share a common purpose—to present the reader with interesting and useful information drawn from primary and/or secondary sources. But whereas essays are intended mainly for a general audience, reports, being more "technical," are aimed at a more specific, more knowledgeable audience. Moreover, report texts are usually organized in sections under subheadings keyed to a table of contents rather than being continuous, like most essays, and they are more likely to contain tables and graphic illustrations.

Report assignments can be of several different kinds. For example, following a field-trip, survey, or interview you may be asked to write an objective account of your findings. Depending on the course and the instructor, you may have to offer your own conclusions.

In business courses, you may have to prepare a report analyzing a business problem or marketing opportunity, putting forward recommendations and perhaps a plan for their implementation. The emphasis is on concise presentation of practical information tightly organized under subheadings. A one-page abstract or "executive summary" precedes the text and provides a brief overview of its content.

Book Report

In some courses, you will read a book and then summarize its content in a book report. Or you may be asked to read several publications—books, articles, reports, etc.—and then outline what the authors said, perhaps evaluating your findings as well.

Summary

In a summary you condense the content of an article or excerpt from a longer work into 20-30 percent (or some other prescribed percentage) of its original length. For instance, you may summarize a 500-word article in 100 to 150 words. *In your own words*, restate only the thesis, main points, and conclusion. Occasionally you may use a term or phrase that cannot be altered without losing an essential meaning. Omit the author's specific examples and illustrations. A summary is a miniature of the original—briefer and simpler. It presents only the main ideas, from the author's point of view, showing that you clearly understand what you have read. *Write as though you are that author.* You should never say, "I think . . ." or "In my opinion . . ." or anything that indicates you are writing from your own point of view. A summary tests your ability to read with understanding, not to judge.

Critique

In some courses, such as Philosophy, you may be asked to criticize (analyze and evaluate) an author's argument or point of view. Begin by summarizing the passage in your own words, showing the various steps the author has taken in building toward a conclusion. If you agree with the overall statement, try to extend it, using your own examples; if you disagree, give good reasons. Some instructors permit the use of the first-person "I" in critique writing.

* * *

Conventions of style vary for different kinds of essays in different disciplines. This manual describes and exemplifies several of the most commonly used styles. When you are given an essay assignment, ask your instructor about which style you should use.

Parts of Essays

Title Page

The *MLA Handbook* says that a separate title page is not needed for research essays. It stipulates that title pages be combined with first text pages, as follows:

Leslie Peeler

Dr. M. Smith

English 128

14 Oct. 1995

Culture Clash: The Impact of European

Settlement on the Kwakiutl

The arrival of European settlers on the Pacific

Northwest coast of North America had a profound impact on the

flourishing and highly sophisticated indigenous cultures

In this example, the student's last name appears half an inch from the top of the page, followed by the page number, and flush with the right margin. This combination of name and page number forms a running headline which appears in the same position on all subsequent pages. Next, the names of the student, instructor, and course, followed by the date, are double spaced beginning one inch from the top of the page and flush with the left margin. The essay title is centred, beginning a double space below the date, and is *not* in all capital letters (the rules for capitalizing are in item 10 on page 53). The first paragraph, indented half an inch or five letter spaces, begins a double space below the title with one-inch margins to left and right.

Note: some instructors may require you to provide a separate title page for research essays as well as for other kinds of essays, too (if you are in doubt, ask). To prepare a separate title page, take a single, unlined sheet of paper and on it place the title of the essay in ALL CAPITAL letters, your name and student registration number, the course and section, your instructor's name, the name of your college or university, and the date. Imitate the order, arrangement, and spacing of the sample layout on page 11. Leave the back of the title page blank.

Title

The title presents the first words a reader encounters, so it is very important. Make it accurate and specific—and, if possible, catchy.

RESEARCH ESSAY

is not a title at all; it merely indicates a general kind of essay.

THE HUDSON'S BAY COMPANY

could be the title of a heavy volume; it has far too much scope for a term paper.

THE HUDSON'S BAY COMPANY AS A COLONIAL POWER,
1670-1770

is better, because it makes a specific promise about the essay's contents. An effective title invites the reader to resolve a conflict, explore a mystery, discover a meaning.

For a term paper, a *subtitle* can help by providing additional information, as in the examples below. Note that both title layouts use a colon to precede the subtitle.

COLLATERAL DAMAGE: HOW MILITARY EUPHEMISMS
AFFECT OUR PERCEPTION OF THE GULF WAR

Note: this subtitle provides further details to explain a vague title and clarify the true subject.

UNBORN DRUNKS:
THE TRAGEDY OF FETAL ALCOHOL SYNDROME

Note: here emotional language suggests an appeal to feelings and social awareness.

Sample Alternative Title Page

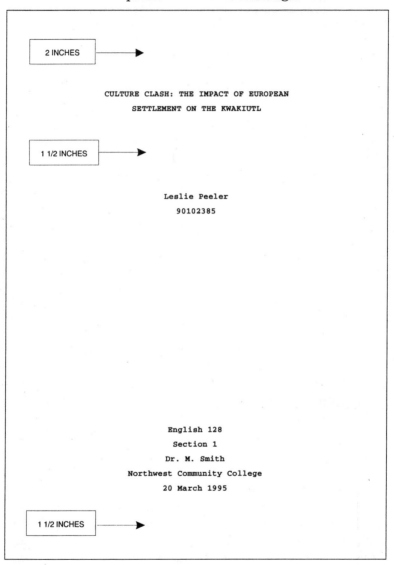

2 INCHES ➤

CULTURE CLASH: THE IMPACT OF EUROPEAN
SETTLEMENT ON THE KWAKIUTL

1 1/2 INCHES ➤

Leslie Peeler
90102385

English 128
Section 1
Dr. M. Smith
Northwest Community College
20 March 1995

1 1/2 INCHES ➤

Perhaps you are writing about a published work and wish to include its title as part of your own. If it is separately published (e.g., a book, film, work of art, play, or television program), underline that part of your title: ANIMAL SYMBOLISM IN FINDLEY'S <u>THE WARS</u> (book); ALLUSIONS TO CHRISTIAN MYTH IN <u>FIELD OF DREAMS</u> (film); THE TRIUMPH OF WOMEN IN ARTEMISIA GENTILLESCHI'S <u>JUDITH BEHEADING HOLOFERNES</u> (painting).

If you include the title of a poem, song, short story, essay, magazine or newspaper article, scholarly paper, or any other *part* of a longer work, place it in double quotation marks: POETIC ELEMENTS IN COHEN'S LYRIC FOR "FAMOUS BLUE RAINCOAT" (song); DECODING THE DECEPTION: ARENDT'S "LYING IN POLITICS" (essay).

Avoid a title that is a complete sentence. Instead, use a phrase—a hint rather than a flat statement. Do not place a period after your title (or any other heading or subheading).

Contents

A table of contents is used only for reports or long essays that require several distinct parts identified by subheadings. It should appear on a separate, unnumbered page, following the title page. It lists the subheadings and their accompanying page numbers. Label the page Contents centred at the top, and word the list and the subheadings in the text identically. If you need a complex system of subdivisions, consult Turabian.

Epigraph

You may wish to put a finishing touch on your essay by attaching an epigraph—a striking, pertinent quotation that helps prepare the reader's mind for the text that immediately follows. For essays with MLA-style title pages, insert the epigraph, centred and double spaced, between the title and the first line of text. For an essay with a separate title page, centre the epigraph three inches from the top of another separate sheet which you then insert between the title page and the first page of text. Do not use quotation marks. Place the name of the author below the epigraph flush right, followed by the title of the work. Do not include bibliographical details about the source of the quotation.

Text

A basic essay expounds *one* main thesis—the idea you wish to prove. Readers generally expect to understand clearly from your *beginning* paragraph what this thesis is (sometimes, however, you may build up to your thesis statement, placing it in a dramatic position later in the text). The *middle* of the essay develops the thesis by providing details, reasons, examples, comparisons, contrasts, definitions, research, or other evidence supporting your main claim. Each paragraph presents *one* aspect of your main idea; it takes one step toward your conclusion in the *ending* paragraph.

Do *not* indicate a new paragraph by leaving an extra line space. Instead, indent the first line of each paragraph *half an inch* or five letter spaces. Double space the text throughout the essay (unless you choose to single space block quotations—see "Lengthy Quotations," page 32.)

An essay text is usually continuous. Still, as noted above, long essays or reports sometimes require subheadings. If so, follow Turabian's advice, and put these in upper and lower case letters, underlined, and centred on the page with an extra line space above.

Illustrations and Tables

A graph, diagram, picture, or table should appear where it most logically fits—preferably right after your first mention of it in the text. Do not include illustrations unless your assignment clearly requires them; and do not include them without introducing them in the text.

If you use several graphs or diagrams, number them with arabic numerals: `Fig. 1`, `Fig. 2`, etc. Place this label *below* the illustration, starting at the left margin; continue on the same line with a simple legend or caption; then add a full citation to indicate the source. Double space the caption if more than one line is needed.

For tables, place the heading `Table` on a line of its own *above* the material and against the left margin; add an arabic numeral if you use more than one table; leave a line space, and start the descriptive caption at the left margin, double spaced if it runs to more than one line; include a full citation immediately *below* the table.

Appendix

An appendix appears at the end of the essay, immediately following the text, under the centred heading `Appendix`. It may include a graph, table, or other documentary material too extensive to put in the body of the essay without breaking its continuity. Indicate an appendix with a parenthetical note in your text at the place you want the reader to refer to it, e.g., `(see Appendix)`. If you use more than one, add arabic numerals to the headings and to the text references, e.g., `(see Appendix 2)`.

Content Notes

Regardless of whether you use MLA style, with source references in your text, or the note style of documentation (see pages 81-87 for discussion and examples), you may also wish to include content notes in your essays. They provide information, comment, or explanation that cannot be accommodated within the text.

To incorporate a single content note (you are documenting with parenthetical text references, not footnotes) place a superscript (half a space above the line) arabic numeral [1] immediately after the item you wish to comment upon. If the note is brief, write it, double spaced, one letter space after a matching numeral at the foot of the same page (see page 82 for layout of footnotes). If the note is lengthy, or is accompanied by other content notes, place it under the heading `Endnotes` on a separate page immediately following the last text page. Number successive notes consecutively throughout the text using arabic superscripts. Here is a sample note:

> [1] As Lewis Mumford says, in <u>Herman Melville</u>, "one might garner a whole book of verse from <u>Moby-Dick</u>" (181). W.O. Matthiessen, in <u>American Renaissance</u> (426), goes further and actually sets out lines in blank verse form.

If you are using the note system of documentation, combine your content notes with your reference notes and number them together. Place the notes at the bottoms of the appropriate pages or, alternatively, gather them as endnotes on a separate page following the text, according to your instructor's requirements.

Use content notes *sparingly*: the information they contain must be of fundamental interest.

Works Cited

This is a list of *all* the sources you referred to in your text, including nonprint sources such as audiotapes, records, films, electronic documents, etc. Whenever you use someone else's work in any way, except to confirm common knowledge, you should supply *both* a text reference *and* a corresponding works cited entry. You must also give a reference for material you have paraphrased but not necessarily quoted; again, a citation is required.

Some instructors expect you to subdivide your list of works cited using appropriate subtitles: "Books," "Articles," "Interviews," etc., or "Primary Sources" and "Secondary Sources." Usually, however, you will simply arrange all the citations in a single, undifferentiated list at the end of the essay under the heading Works Cited. (See pages 52-55 for a description of how to present entries in works cited.)

Presentation of Essays

During your first year or two in college, your instructors will probably accept hand-written essays, but later on they will undoubtedly expect them to be typed. So, if you are unable to type or use a word processor, you should seriously consider learning how (or be prepared to pay for the service). A word of warning, though: don't type your essays until you have developed a reasonable level of proficiency; don't use your essays for typing practice.

It is not just a matter of turning out well-presented papers. When you acquire adequate keyboard skills, you will be able to speed up the writing process and make it more effective. It is a waste of study time to laboriously type up a text you have already hand written and revised. Instead, you should compose directly onto the machine to produce a cleaner text that is easier to edit. The word processor in particular allows, indeed encourages, the use of a variety of editing techniques—see the following section, "Word Processing Tips."

Even if you use a typewriter, you can manipulate your text using scissors and Scotch tape, cutting and pasting physically rather than electronically, and then photocopying the revised version. Typing facilitates editing, as well as producing a better looking text.

Appearance *is* important. A well-presented essay gives the reader confidence that the writer has essential aspects of the writing process under control.

Be sure to proofread your text carefully. When typewriting, use correction fluid or a correction tape when making minor text changes. For last-minute corrections, use the proofreader's symbols shown on page 19 (your instructor may use them when marking your essay).

1. Use 8½ x 11 inch paper.
2. Do not present an essay written in pencil. Write, or type, on one side of the page only. Leave the other side blank.
3. Double space the lines of text, whether you type, use a word processor, or write by hand.

4. If you use a word processor, be sure your printer is of reasonable quality (avoid the cheaper kinds of dot-matrix printers). Remember to keep a copy of the essay on a back-up disk. Word processing programs vary—stick as closely as your program will allow to the conventions given in this manual.

5. When using a word processor, left justify the text, leaving the right margin "ragged." Make sure the print in your text is sharp and black; it must be easy to read (and photocopy).

6. Use blank paper for typed essays, lined paper for hand-written ones. Use blank paper for diagrams, tables, and title pages.

7. When page numbering an MLA-style research essay, use running headlines containing your last name and the page number set flush against the right margin (see the sample on page 18). However, depending on the kind of essay you are writing, and the level of the course for which it is required, you may not need to follow research-essay style (if in doubt, consult your instructor). In which case, prepare a separate title page (see page 10 for guidelines); then count but *do not put the number on* the first text page (page 2 of the text is thus the first numbered page). Omit your name, and either centre the page number or place it against the right margin. For both types of essays, number the pages consecutively, including pages for endnotes, appendices, and works cited. Do not punctuate the numbers.

8. Many instructors like to receive essays that are stapled in the top left-hand corner; some prefer a folder (in which case put your name, the course, and the section number on the outside cover). The *MLA Handbook* suggests the use of paper clips (but they are not very secure). If in doubt, ask.

9. If you present your essay in a folder, leave a 1½-inch margin at the left side of the page to allow for hole punching. Leave a 1-inch margin elsewhere. If you staple or paper clip the pages at the top left-hand corner, leave a 1-inch margin all round. See the sample on page 18, and try to achieve a similar effect.

10. If you type or hand write your essay, make a photocopy and keep it safe—it is rare, but not unknown, for instructors to lose students' essays.

Sample Text Page

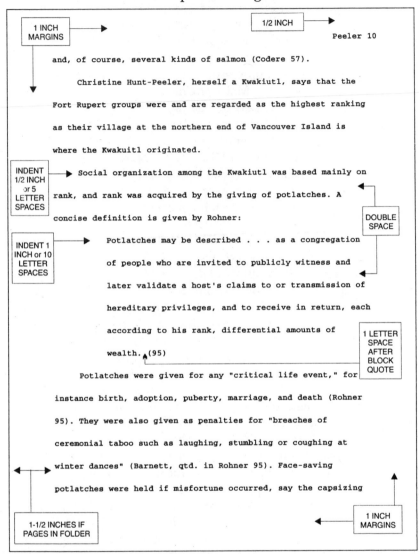

1 INCH MARGINS

1/2 INCH

and, of course, several kinds of salmon (Codere 57).

Christine Hunt-Peeler, herself a Kwakiutl, says that the Fort Rupert groups were and are regarded as the highest ranking as their village at the northern end of Vancouver Island is where the Kwakuitl originated.

INDENT 1/2 INCH or 5 LETTER SPACES

Social organization among the Kwakiutl was based mainly on rank, and rank was acquired by the giving of potlatches. A concise definition is given by Rohner:

DOUBLE SPACE

INDENT 1 INCH or 10 LETTER SPACES

Potlatches may be described . . . as a congregation of people who are invited to publicly witness and later validate a host's claims to or transmission of hereditary privileges, and to receive in return, each according to his rank, differential amounts of wealth. (95)

1 LETTER SPACE AFTER BLOCK QUOTE

Potlatches were given for any "critical life event," for instance birth, adoption, puberty, marriage, and death (Rohner 95). They were also given as penalties for "breaches of ceremonial taboo such as laughing, stumbling or coughing at winter dances" (Barnett, qtd. in Rohner 95). Face-saving potlatches were held if misfortune occurred, say the capsizing

1-1/2 INCHES IF PAGES IN FOLDER

1 INCH MARGINS

This sample page is a guide for the final draft of an MLA-style research essay employing parenthetical references. It shows the page number (i.e., page 10) as part of the running headline. (Ask your instructor if you need to follow this particular convention.) The text is *double* spaced as is the block quotation which is indented one inch (or ten letter spaces) from the left margin. Note the text references and the placement of the parentheses. The Hunt-Peeler reference in the second paragraph is to an interview, so no page number appears.

Here are some of the most commonly used proofreader's symbols to aid you in the final correcting of your text:

Margin Symbol: *Text Symbol:*

                                    or
                          insert word phrase
                                    ∧

$\mathcal{G}$ delete ~~word or~~ phrase

                          change
                          ~~correct~~ a word or phrase

                          move a word or phrase (misplaced)

stet   restore ~~original~~ text

L.c.   make /ower case

                          close up sp⁀ace

separate/words (add space)

trs   transpose letters words or

¶   begin new paragraph

no ¶   no new paragraph

Word Processing Tips

The use of computers and word processing software can be of enormous help in the preparation of essays. Full-featured word processors, in combination with sophisticated printers, offer a multitude of options. These tools will not magically transform you into a better writer, but they can certainly help with the rewriting and formatting of your work. Here are some guidelines for users of word processors:

1. Take the time to learn your software, especially its editing and formatting features. Simple cut, copy, and paste routines can speed rewriting and rearranging of text. Page formats (including details such as margin setting) and paragraph styles (specifying indentation, spacing, and alignment) can be defined. Once established, these definitions can be saved and used repeatedly on future papers. In the long run, you will not regret spending some time with your software manuals and reading the "help" information provided with the program.

2. Use a standard, mono-spaced typeface or font, such as Courier. (Courier is used in the sample essay pages in this book.) This kind of font allots equal space to all letters and characters.

3. Leave your right margins "ragged," as both MLA and APA style guidelines require. Your instructor may permit justified text (where lines of text align with the page margins on both sides), but if you adopt this style, *never* use it in conjunction with a mono-spaced font. Often the result is large and unsightly gaps between words. Instead, use a proportionally spaced font, such as Times Roman, which allots space on the basis of letter width and can adjust spacing between words and between letters. Stay away from fancy script or other "designer" fonts which are inappropriate for text.

4. You may or may not hyphenate words at the ends of lines—it is up to you. If you choose to, however, you should let the computer do it by using your software's automatic hyphenation options (if available) or by running a hyphenation routine when your writing and revising is complete. Do not type a hyphen and a "hard return" in the middle of a word mid-way

through a paragraph. If you do that, and then revise the first part of the paragraph, you may end up creating short lines ending with unwanted hyphens later in the paragraph, which will have to be corrected. (Note that APA style does not allow end-of-line hyphenation if a paper is to be submitted for publication to an APA journal.)

5. Your program and printer may be capable of producing italic type which is usually used instead of underlining in published material. The MLA discourages this practice in essay writing, while the APA is ambivalent (unless you are submitting an article for publication, in which case it is not permitted). Do not use italics without consulting your instructor. Your software will accomplish underlining as easily as italicization, so you might as well underline and be done with it.

6. All full-featured word processing programs include a spell-checking feature. Always use it, but never rely on it completely. If only one typographical error is found and corrected, it is worth the time, and you will be a little closer to the always elusive goal of a "letter-perfect" paper. But the spell-checking software cannot be a substitute for your own careful proofreading. The computer will not notice that you typed "form" instead of "from," or "too" instead of "two."

If your software permits it, learn how to build a custom dictionary. This can be especially helpful if you are writing a number of papers about similar subjects. Your custom dictionary can hold a variety of specific terms and proper nouns which appear frequently in your writing but are not in the program's main dictionary. Then, the software will ignore those "custom" words, and the spell-checking process will be faster.

7. Always, always, *always* make back-up copies of your work. Typically, you will store your essay on the computer's hard disk. While writing, frequently save your work to the disk. Whenever you finish a session on the computer, also save a copy of your work to a diskette. Should the computer or the hard-disk drive malfunction, your work can be retrieved from the diskette using another machine. If you are working on a lengthy paper that may go through a series of drafts, you may want to keep separate back-up copies of each major revision. That way, material used in your first draft, but discarded in the second draft, can always be reinstated in your third draft.

Handling Mechanical Details

In polishing your final draft, pay close attention to the many mechanical details that need to be checked. For full discussion and exemplification of them, see the *MLA Handbook*. Meanwhile, here are some items that regularly draw criticism when mishandled.

1. Spell out round numbers that can be expressed in one or two words (e.g., eight, twenty-seven, two hundred), and use numerals for the rest (e.g., 8½, 127, 3,420). Spell out a number that begins a sentence. Retain numerals where they occur in names or titles (e.g., 49th Avenue). Use numerals also for dates, times, measurements, and money. Avoid mixing numerals and spelled-out numbers (use all numerals, e.g., 8½ by 11, not 8½ by eleven).

2. In science essays, decimal numbers less than 1 should be preceded by a zero (e.g. 0.563, not .563).

3. The simplest way to write a date is 4 July 1976. Write 62 BC, but AD 62.

4. Underline the title of a book, magazine, newspaper, film, play, opera, long poem, tape, radio or television program, or record album. Use *quotation marks* to indicate a part within a whole: a chapter, story, article, essay, aria, short poem, or song title. Underline foreign words that are not part of our ordinary speech: underline "Weltschmerz," but not "milieu." See page 21 for a discussion of underlining vs. italics.

5. Use abbreviations in your notes and works cited entries, but avoid them in your text, except for conventional forms such as "a.m.," "Mr.," "RCMP," and "UN." In your text, spell out the names of months and measurements such as "inch," "pound," and "metre." Except in well-known cases (such as NATO), spell out the name of an organization on first use, and place the abbreviation in a parenthesis immediately after—e.g., Canadian International Development Agency (CIDA); thereafter use the abbreviation alone. Punctuate abbreviations with care. Omit periods in capitalized abbreviations, but include periods

with lower-case abbreviations (see examples above). If in doubt, consult the *MLA Handbook*.

6. Avoid contractions. Write "do not" instead of "don't"; "cannot" instead of "can't," etc. Your tone is thus more formal, a desirable effect in most essays.

7. Misuse of the possessive apostrophe is annoying. None of the personal pronouns needs an apostrophe. The word "it's" means either "it is" or "it has." The proper form of this possessive pronoun is "its."

8. The general rule is to add 's to the singular of *any* possessive noun (the cat's collar, Mr. Jones's house), but an apostrophe alone to the plural if it ends in *s* (the cats' collars, the Joneses' house). Plural nouns that do *not* end in *s* form the possessive by adding 's (children's).

9. The convention for using apostrophes with names ending in *s* is variable. Some writers will call an essay by George Williams "Williams' essay"; others, "Williams's essay." The latter is preferable since the former, read aloud, sounds like "William's essay"—which is wrong. If a possessive form sounds awkward aloud, consider using a prepositional phrase: instead of "Jesus's wisdom," write "the wisdom of Jesus."

10. Learn the basic rules of punctuation thoroughly. Whether it seems fair or not, grammar and punctuation—they are closely related—greatly influence your reader's response to your work. Faulty or irregular punctuation can be confusing, and may lead a reader to underestimate your ideas.

11. Bad spelling is distracting, and an otherwise good essay is likely to be penalized for it. Take responsibility for your spelling errors. Develop a list of misspelled words; review that list when you proofread your final draft. Use the spell checker on your word processor, but do not rely on it alone (see item 6 on page 21). Buy a good dictionary and consult it whenever you doubt your spelling.

Avoiding Discriminatory Language

Nowadays readers, writers, publishers, and teachers are increasingly sensitive to evidences of bias in written language. As a courtesy to your reader, and as part of your social responsibility as a writer, you should avoid language that discriminates against other people with respect to their gender, race, social class, sexual orientation, and religious beliefs.

The English language contains a built-in bias in favour of males, but the convention that says "a person" is always "he" can easily be amended. In some cases, the phrase "he or she" may be substituted. Often a switch to the plural will circumvent the problem. You should adopt these and other similar usages including gender neutral nouns (e.g. "worker" instead of "workman," "flight attendant" instead of "stewardess") to ensure that, unwittingly, you do not offend your reader by an inappropriate choice of words.

Avoiding Plagiarism

Avoid plagiarism. It is something you consciously or unconsciously "commit" when using the words or ideas of another person as though they were your own—a sort of literary sin.

When, without acknowledgment, you (1) "use another person's ideas or expressions in your writing," (2) incorporate someone's "particularly apt term," (3) find yourself "paraphrasing another's argument," or (4) adopt someone else's "line of thinking," you have committed plagiarism (Gibaldi 26).

Note the quotation marks and documentation in the preceding sentence. You, too, *must* acknowledge by means of conventional text references, or appropriate notes, your borrowing of someone else's words, ideas, data, or other information. Penalties for plagiarism can be severe. If you suspect you are plagiarizing, you probably are, as your instructor will easily recognize. Ironically it is easier and more impressive to show off your well-chosen sources than to try to conceal them.

When you find secondary material you want to use in your essay, there are three ways to incorporate it: by *paraphrase, summary,* or *quotation,* accompanied in each case by an appropriate text reference. Since all three are vital components of research papers, and since each is susceptible to plagiarism, they deserve separate consideration.

Read the following excerpt taken from page 2 of the introduction to *A Casebook of Ideologies,* by Macdonald Burbidge:

> A reader should also be aware of the distinction between empirical claims—that is, those which describe what *is, was* or *will be the case,* and which can be tested by observation, experience, and experiment—and moral claims, which are claims about what *ought to be the case,* and which are grounded upon some type of moral principle. For example, one may point out the empirical fact that ordinary people in Chile do not have freedom of speech, since it is empirically observable that if they do speak out, they may be flung in jail. But those who claim that Chileans ought to be free to speak without fear of punishment are making a moral claim, and it therefore makes sense to ask them for the conclusive principle upon which the claim is based. For example, it could be based upon the Christian view that God has willed that humans be free, the utilitarian view that such freedom will in the long run lead to the maximization of happiness, or an *a priori* (self-evident) claim, such as might be made by a follower of Kant, that each person has a moral right to free speech regardless of the law. (Emphasis added.)

Now, observe the use and misuse of this material in the sections that follow.

Paraphrase

This term signifies the restatement of a short passage in other words.

REASONS TO EMPLOY PARAPHRASES
1. You are more concerned with the original author's points than with the actual words—substance rather than style.
2. Too much quotation clutters the page; paraphrase provides variety, an alternative way of incorporating a source.
3. Your own expression, or "voice," should dominate the essay.

FORM OF PARAPHRASES

1. Use mainly short passages of paraphrase (one or two sentences), combining them with quotations and your own comments.
2. Try to parallel the structure, content, and length of the original.
3. It is not acceptable to repeat the original and merely alter or cut a few words; instead, rephrase all the information *in your own words*.
4. Handle a key word, startling phrase, highly technical, or untranslatable term by *quoting* it.
5. Maintain a similar level of diction; the paraphrase should not be a watered-down version of the original.

Note: in special kinds of essays such as book reports and scientific research reports, paraphrase and summary may comprise a major component of the writing. An excellent place to find examples of combined paraphrase, summary, and quotation is in any volume of "Abstracts" in the reference section of the library.

In regular essays, you should paraphrase the more routine material in the original source, and quote only the most striking, significant statements. They will then stand out against a background of paraphrase. If you quote too much, the impact of individual quotations is weakened. You should therefore differentiate the more important statements (quotations) from the less important (paraphrases).

PARAPHRASE OF THE TWO HIGHLIGHTED SENTENCES ON THE PREVIOUS PAGE

```
Burbidge states that a person is making a "moral
claim" when he or she asserts the right of all
people to speak with impunity. Such a claim might be
rooted in the spiritual belief that free speech is a
right bestowed by a Higher Power; in the pragmatic
belief that this liberty will produce "the
maximization of happiness"; or in the Kantian belief
that, beyond the bounds of any instituted authority,
```

free speech is the inherent right of every human being—an "a priori" truth (2).

This is an acceptable paraphrase, containing just three quoted key phrases. It restates all of the principal ideas of the passage, maintaining the basic order, integrity, and force of the original while recasting it in a fresh way. A parenthetical page reference accompanies the mention of the author's name in the text to acknowledge the source of the paraphrased ideas. By turning to the works cited page, the reader will find this citation:

Burbidge, Macdonald. A Casebook of Ideologies: Liberalism, Communism, Meritocracy, Conservatism, Democratic Socialism, Anarchism. Vancouver, BC: Vancouver Community College Press, 1990.

With this information, the reader could then go to the library and find the book, turn to page 2, and read more. Without this reference and corresponding citation, the author of the above paraphrase is guilty of plagiarism: the ideas have been "borrowed" without acknowledgment.

Summary

A summary is a condensation of a longer passage. A whole book could be summarized in a sentence, a chapter in a paragraph. It all depends on how much detail you wish to retain. The entire original selection above might be summarized as follows:

Burbidge distinguishes between empirical and moral claims, emphasizing that they differ significantly. Whereas the former rely solely upon perception and scientific measurement to describe objective reality, the latter rely on idealisms or felt certainties about what reality should or might be. Under an oppressive regime, freedom of speech is forbidden to most people, as the empiricist observes. In contrast, says Burbidge, the moralist witnesses the often severe violation of fundamental human rights and makes judgments based on deep religious, pragmatic, or "<u>a priori</u>" principles (2).

Introducing the author at the beginning, repeating the name as a reminder later on, and concluding with the page reference is a simple way to frame a paraphrase or summary, distinguishing it from the rest of the text and acknowledging its source. Thus you avoid plagiarism. See pages 42-51 for explanation of the content and placement of references to sources.

Quotation

The term *quotation* refers to your use of the *actual words* of another person, whether from a printed text, a lecture, an electronic source, etc. You must distinguish his or her words from your own by using quotation marks or other conventions (described below in "Quoting Effectively"). Quotation without acknowledgment, however, produces plagiarism, as in the following example:

The moral issue of free speech is particularly important today, especially in countries where people are flung in jail or even killed just for speaking out against the regime. There are different reasons free speech is morally right and ought to be the case, based on conclusive principles. The Christian idea is that God wants us to be free; a utilitarian thinker believes that happiness will be maximized; others believe the self-evident idea of Kant, that everyone has "a moral right to freedom of speech" no matter what the law says.

This is a mishmash of plagiarisms. The writer has copied the pattern of thinking of the original, used quotation without employing quotation marks, misquoted a phrase, and paraphrased extensively—all without crediting the source. The quotation marks hint at the writer's good intentions, but half measures are not enough. To make matters worse, Kant has been misrepresented.

In contrast, the presence of summary statements, paraphrases, and quotations, accompanied by appropriate documentation, will lend credibility and the force of authority to the main points of your research essay.

Often individual sentences will contain three kinds of language: your own words (introducing the topic, drawing conclusions, etc.), paraphrase or summary (source material expressed in your words), and direct quotation (word for word from the original). These three make a powerful combination.

Quoting Effectively

Often our reading inspires us to respond in writing; our ideas and expression are profoundly stimulated, guided, and even formed by the words of others. To invite the thought and language of other writers into our own work affirms our participation with other minds in the ceaseless effort to make sense of things. Our writing becomes more interesting and complex.

Purpose

In many courses, especially in the humanities and social sciences, the instructor expects your essays to reflect your reading. Quotations from respected authors in the discipline add variety and authority to your essay by introducing another voice or point of view, illustrating major points, and reinforcing your arguments. Find the strongest quotations you can—surprising details, vivid statements of controversy, prime examples, and insightful phrases and sentences that seem to condense a large idea into a memorable truth.

Note: since you have to provide references and corresponding citations for all quotations, it is essential that you make notes painstakingly when doing library research. Use quotation marks to distinguish quotations from paraphrase or summary; record page numbers for each quotation; use ellipsis periods (see page 34) to indicate omissions.

How Much Quotation?

Avoid very long quotations, especially in a short essay. Quote only key passages. Make sure you know the desired balance between quotation and text. In English essays, usually 10-15 percent of the text is quotation, but a research essay or book report may require more. Ask your instructor. Excessive quotation suggests you are not doing enough of your own thinking; too little indicates you have not done the research.

References for Quotations

If a word, phrase, or sentence deserves to be quoted, it also requires a reference. Provide a reference for *all* quotations, even brief ones. Typically, a reference includes an author's name and a page number. The name may appear in your sentence or in a parenthesis; the page number *always* appears in a parenthesis. (See "Sample References," pages 46-51). When several successive quotations are taken from the same page, a single parenthesis after the last quotation of a series refers to all the quotations following the preceding reference.

Brief Quotations

Incorporate brief quotations—key words, phrases, or sentences—as smoothly as possible *within* your own sentences. Place quotation marks around them:

```
Lawrence called the novel the "one bright book of
life" (126), elevating it above all other forms of
literature.
```

Note: the quotation is a natural grammatical element of the sentence, needing only the quotation marks and the reference. Avoid using phrases such as "In the following quotation" or "as shown in this quote" since the quotation marks already indicate you are quoting.

A quotation can appear at the beginning, middle, or end of your sentence. Try to provide variety:

```
"The horror! The horror!"--this is Kurtz's last
judgment (608).
```

```
Atwood opposes any theory that limits expression:
"Theory is a positive force when it vitalizes and
enables, but a negative one when it is used to
amputate and repress, to create a batch of
self-righteous rules and regulations" (24).
```

Note: use a colon after a *complete* statement that introduces a quotation.

After phrases such as "so-and-so says," "she writes," "the report claims," "the law states," etc., which are not complete statements, use a comma to introduce the quotation that follows:

```
Vidal says, "of all writers, the one who does not
mind anonymity is the one most apt to appeal to an
ambitious [film] director" (139).
```

Omit this comma if you introduce the quotation with the word "that":

```
Vidal says that "of all writers, the one who does
not mind . . ." (139).
```

You may subordinate a quotation by placing it in a parenthesis. The page number is in *square brackets* to show a parenthesis within a parenthesis:

```
Ruskin answers the initial questions ("How does one
define children's literature?" and "How has the
language of children's literature changed?" [214])
with a good deal of humour.
```

Use a pair of dashes, instead of parentheses or commas, as a way of emphasizing whatever is between them, including quoted material:

Ruskin is firm in her stand that many fairy tales,
nonsense poems, and folk legends--"originally
intended for an audience of any age at all"
(215)--prove there is continuity between childhood
and adulthood.

Lengthy Quotations

Quotations that would comprise five or more lines of prose on your page should be distinguished visually from the rest of the text. The *MLA Handbook* advocates the following: after one line space, begin on a new line, and indent the quotation one inch, or ten spaces, from the left margin. Double space the text of the quotation (see the example on page 18). If the quotation includes the first line of a paragraph, indent that line a further quarter inch, or three spaces, to indicate the paragraph break.

Do not use quotation marks around an indented quotation unless they appear in the original source. In general, introduce such lengthy, and by implication important, quotations with a complete statement followed by a colon:

While this movement in art was a rebellion against
morbid, academic values, Ernst Fischer is critical
of it:

> Impressionism, dissolving the world of
> light, breaking it up into colours,
> recording it as a sequence of sensory
> perceptions, became more and more
> expressive of a very complex, very
> short-term subject-object relationship.
> The individual, reduced to loneliness,
> concentrating on himself, experiences the
> world as a set of nerve stimuli,
> impressions, and moods, as a "shimmering

```
chaos," as "my" experience, "my"

sensation. (71)

In a world that is increasingly fragmented and

dehumanized, the role of art as a force for

achieving political awareness . . .
```

This example shows a complete statement, followed by a colon, introducing a lengthy, indented quotation. Quotation marks appear only because they occur in Fischer's text. An additional indenting of a quarter of an inch, or three spaces, indicates Fischer's paragraphing. For indented quotations, the parenthetical page reference goes *outside* the final sentence period after *one* letter space.

In some courses, for some instructors, you may be required to follow an older convention for presenting lengthy quotations. In this case, you leave a line space before and after the quotation which you *single space* and indent half an inch, or five spaces, from the left margin. Single spacing produces a block quotation (Turabian's preferred style) that is more in keeping with the design of printed books. If in doubt, ask your instructor which style you should use.

Common Faults

Do not sprinkle your text with quotations arbitrarily. Do not try to make a quotation serve as the grammatical subject of a sentence (e.g., `"Art will disappear as life gains more equilibrium"` proves what `Mondrian` means). Do not insert space after opening or before closing quotation marks. Do not let a quotation stand on its own as an independent sentence; instead, introduce it with your own comment, perhaps mentioning the author's name. In every case, your own sentence must in some way surround the quotation, making it a coherent, natural part of your text. (Test whether or not a quotation fits by reading your whole sentence aloud, including the quotation.) Use quotations to back up your *main* points; do not quote unimportant matters of fact. A quotation should always *add to* the logical development of your discussion, not merely repeat it in different words.

Ellipsis

The ellipsis consists of three spaced periods . . . that indicate the omission of one or more words from a quotation. Do *not* put an ellipsis at the beginnings or ends of short quotations (single words or brief phrases), since they are self-evidently incomplete:

```
The book sets out to define "dehumanization" and
what Marcuse repeatedly calls the "one-dimensional
man" (16).
```

Always use an ellipsis when you omit a word or words from *within* a quotation:

```
Lawrence states, "Freud is the starting point . . .
in any study of the mind" (78).
```

Use an ellipsis *to end* a quoted fragment of reasonable length that occurs at the end of your sentence. In such a case, the order of items is: beginning quotation marks, quotation, ellipsis, ending quotation marks, parenthetical reference, and final period:

```
Lawrence goes on to say, "Indeed, we find in Freud
our first true pioneer of the unconscious . . ."
(80).
```

Leave a letter space between the last word of the quotation and the first period of the ellipsis.

Use an ellipsis *to introduce a block quotation* that does not begin with a sentence capital. An ellipsis is also necessary at the end of a block quotation which does not end with a period in the original; in this case, use four periods as shown here, with the page number set apart after one letter space:

```
In their introduction, Cunningham and Reich
encourage us to slow down, to become contemplative
as we approach artistic and literary works, because
it would
             . . . help all of us to savor once again
          the power of language and image. That
          would be a great boon for ordinary life.
```

```
It would enrich us, and . . . help us to

be warily skeptical of the almost

universal abuse of language and the

shallowness of much of our artificial

environment. . . . (3)
```

When you omit one or more sentences from *within* a quotation, use an ellipsis. *A complete sentence* of quotation must precede and follow the ellipsis, however. After the sentence period, place three spaced periods, leave another space, and continue with the balance of the quotation:

```
Thouless maintains that "We are allowing our brains

to degenerate into mere mechanisms when they were

meant for plasticity and change. . . . Inflexibility

of mind would lead to the extermination of the human

race" (129).
```

Do *not*, however, use the three spaced periods to stitch together statements from widely separated areas of the text. The effect is quite misleading. Use your own words to link them.

Brackets

Use square brackets when you must alter, or add, a word or phrase within a quotation to make the quotation fit grammatically, or to supply a proper name to a pronoun lacking a clear antecedent:

```
The same critic writes, "When we first meet him

[Hamlet], a spirit of gloom prevails . . ." (41).
```

Use this device only when you have to. Almost any sentence can be rewritten to incorporate the quotation as it originally appears, or the quotation can be trimmed to eliminate the offending word or phrase:

```
The same critic writes that when the audience first

encounters Hamlet, "a spirit of gloom prevails" (41).
```

Errors in Quotations

Occasionally you may come across a serious factual or style error, or a spelling mistake, in a quotation you plan to use. If you wish to draw attention to the error, place the Latin word "sic" (meaning "thus") in square brackets after it, as in the following example:

```
According to J. N. Sullivan, "At the time of writing
Moby Dick [sic] the problem that was to haunt
Melville was, as it were, fairly straightforward"
(15).
```

The reader will thus understand that the errors in the title *Moby-Dick* (the lack of italics and a hyphen) occurred in the original source.

Quotation Within a Quotation

In block quotations, preserve quotation marks exactly as they appear in the original—do not supply marks of your own. But when you incorporate a short quotation into your sentence, and any part of that quotation contains double quotation marks, change them to *single* ones.

Original:

Hopkins's invention of what he called "sprung rhythm," "instress," and "inscape" provided a sense of liberation to early twentieth-century poets.

Your sentence:

```
Ezra Pound is one of many poets who found "a sense
of liberation" in "Hopkins's invention of what he
called 'sprung rhythm,' 'instress,' and 'inscape'"
(Markham 61).
```

Note: generally, your quotation marks take precedence over the original ones. In the above example, you are quoting both Markham and Hopkins, and so you need both double and single marks to distinguish the original authors. But if you wanted to quote only Hopkins's term(s) and include nothing from Markham, it would *not* be necessary to use more than your own quotation marks.

Incorrect:

```
Hopkins called this new concept "'instress'"
because . . .
```

Correct:

```
Hopkins called this concept "instress" because . . .
```

Stated as a rule: when you are quoting any one speaker or author, use regular quotation marks. Do not use single quotation marks unless a second speaker intervenes. Note, too, that quotation marks appear around each individual word and phrase in the series quoted above. They are not lumped together as "sprung rhythm, instress, and inscape" because they do not appear together that way in the original source.

Punctuating the Close of Quotations

All punctuation that appears immediately before your closing quotation marks must be grammatical. Thus you do not always have to quote the writer's punctuation, but instead may sometimes supply your own. Your period or comma should go *inside* the quotation marks, unless a parenthetical reference is necessary, in which case your punctuation follows the parenthesis. You should retain the author's question mark or exclamation mark, but not the author's colon, semicolon, or dash when it appears at the end of a quotation.

Original:

. . . they are wise and aware; they enjoy life with gusto, yet face and accept death; they not only work productively but creatively, and they obviously love their fellow human beings . . .

Your sentence:

```
The author admires people who are "wise and aware,"
who "enjoy life with gusto," and who "accept death";
```

```
to him truly sane people function "productively" and
"creatively"; most importantly, they "love their
fellow human beings" (Peck 125).
```

Original:

> Are we to consider individuals healthy simply because they are
> not in pain—no matter how much havoc and harm they bring
> to their fellow human beings?

Your sentence:

```
Peck asks, "Are we to consider individuals healthy
. . . no matter how much havoc and harm they bring
to their fellow human beings?" (125).
```

Your sentence:

```
Can we trust Peck's analysis of "how much harm they
[evil people] bring to their fellow human beings"
(125)?
```

Note: your punctuation takes precedence over the original. In the second example, your question mark rules the sentence, not Peck's.

Quoting Poetry

Incorporate a line or part of a line of poetry as though you were quoting prose. For example,

```
Williams's poem is about "how to perform a funeral."
```

Page and line references are unnecessary when you quote from short poems. Simply acknowledge your source in a footnote (see "The Note Style of Documentation" beginning on page 81).

For a quotation of two or three lines, indicate line endings with a slash:

```
From the start, Williams's poem is didactic,

promising some kind of ethical lesson: "I will teach

you my townspeople / how to perform a funeral."
```

Leave a letter space before and after the slash. Note that there is no slash at the beginning or end of the quotation. To indicate a stanza break, use a pair of slashes // without an extra space between them.

When you quote more than three lines, use *block* form, indented one inch or ten letter spaces from the left margin:

```
One passage in particular demonstrates his

individual sense of rhythm:

        To you

                I can risk words about this

        Mastering them you know

                they are dull

                        servants

        Who say less

        and worse

                than we feel
```

In a block quotation from a poem, try to duplicate the layout of the original as closely as possible, imitating the poet's margins, spacing, punctuation, and any peculiarities of typography.

Long lines of poetry require special treatment in block form. To make more room, indent the first line half an inch or five letter spaces and run it to the right margin; indent the overflow on your next line(s) a further quarter of an inch or three letter spaces. What you have shown as two or more lines will thus be understood to be a single line in the original.

Use of Single Quotation Marks

As well as showing a quotation within a quotation, single quotation marks can indicate your ironic use of someone else's term. You may use such marks (sparingly) to stand for a phrase like "so-called":

```
The shelves were stocked with 'natural' food
products.
```

Use of Italics in Quotations

Any word, phrase, or complete sentence that appears in italics in the original source should be underlined in your quotation.

Original:

To start at the end first, *the peak-experience is only good and desirable, and is never experienced as evil or undesirable.*

Your sentence:

```
Maslow begins by claiming that "peak-experience is
only good and desirable" (76).
```

If you wish to emphasize a word or phrase in a quotation, you may underline it, but only if you include a special phrase in acknowledgment:

```
Daily life, to Lawrence, is merely a facade; the
true life is actually to be found in the
"subterranean regions of the soul" and in the
"primitive" conscious life of the body (94, emphasis
added).
```

Quoting Drama

For brief drama quotations, treat prose dialogue as if it were from a short story or novel, and introduce the name of the character in your sentence. In block quotations of dialogue, indent one inch or ten letter spaces as usual. Begin with the speaker's name, followed by a colon and the dialogue. Omit any stage directions unless pertinent.

```
is characterized by constant tension and bickering:

     Charley: Don't get insulted.

     Willy: Don't insult me.

     Charley: I don't see no sense in it. . . .

(43)
```

For verse drama, follow the convention for references described in "References to Classic Literary Works," page 49.

Acknowledging Sources

Whenever you quote other people's actual words, paraphrase their ideas, or make use of their data or original information, you must acknowledge your indebtedness—both in your text, by using references, and in a list of works cited. Together these two forms of documentation are sufficient for your readers to appreciate the variety and quality of your sources, and to locate them for the purposes of their own research.

Purpose of References

Provide text references (see below for examples) either *within your sentences*, or *in parentheses*, or in combination:

1. to indicate the source, including page number(s) for printed materials, of any quotation you include in your text;
2. to acknowledge your indebtedness for factual information and for ideas paraphrased, or summarized (i.e. not directly quoted), from any source;
3. and to direct readers to the list of works cited for complete details of publication.

Content of References to Printed Sources

A text reference to a printed source *must* contain the following:

1. the last name of the author—*either* in your sentence, *or* as the first item in a parenthesis that follows any quotation, paraphrase, or summary you used;
2. the title of the work, *either* in your sentence, *or* in a parenthesis—*if* you have referred to *more than one work* by the same author;
3. the page number(s) *in a parenthesis* for any quotation, paraphrase, or summary you used.

The content of a parenthetical reference usually takes one of the three following forms:

(87)	—page number alone, when you have already identified the work in your sentence
(Breit 87)	—author's last name (no punctuation following) and page number
(Breit, Writer 87)	—author's last name, comma, title (abbreviated from The Writer Observed, a book, hence underlined) and page number

With few exceptions (the Bible, an encyclopedia, a dictionary, or a one-page article), every parenthetical reference to a printed source will contain a page number. Do not mention page numbers elsewhere in your sentences. For anonymous works, the title (usually abbreviated) replaces the author's name in the parenthesis.

Remember, the parenthesis should *not* repeat details already given in your sentence.

References in Sentences or in Parentheses?

You have a choice: include references either in the body of your sentences or in parentheses. This flexibility allows you to achieve different effects.

1. Einstein and Infeld introduce their history of modern physics as though they were fiction writers: "In imagination there exists the perfect mystery story" (Evolution 3).

This sentence emphasizes the *authors* rather than the source. The inclusion of the abbreviated title in the parenthesis indicates that more than one work by these authors has been referred to, and reveals the specific source of the quotation.

2. In The Evolution of Physics, a layman's guide to physics from Galileo to quantum mechanics and relativity theory, Einstein and Infeld distinguish between Arthur Conan Doyle's and their own "detective novel" (4).

43

This sentence draws attention to the *text*, as well as mentioning the authors, suggesting that the book itself is central to the discussion.

3. Few would argue with the theory that "Human thought creates an ever-changing picture of the universe" (Einstein and Infeld 9).

Here the sentence is more concerned with the *idea* than with the source; thus the authors are subordinated in the parenthesis.

4. Some modern physicists (e.g., Einstein and Infeld) approach their discipline as though it were a creative art or a special branch of philosophy.

Since Einstein and Infeld are just two among many, their names are subordinated, and because nothing has been quoted or paraphrased, there is no page reference.

The point is that the content of your reference may vary according to what element you wish to stress in the sentence.

Placement of Parentheses

In the majority of cases, it is appropriate to place the parenthesis at the end of the sentence in which the reference (paraphrase, summary, or quotation) occurs. It goes *inside* your period but *outside* any ending quotation marks, as in the examples below:

Like most authorities, Zinsser emphasizes that unity is one of the bases of effective writing (46).

According to Zinsser, unity satisfies the reader's "subconscious need for order" (46).

Sometimes, however, you may end the reference part way through the sentence and then introduce a new reference or a comment of your own. In such cases, you should place the parenthesis inside the punctuation at the end of the clause in which the reference appears:

```
Unity is one of the bases of effective writing
(Zinsser 46); it is not, however, easy to achieve.
```

If you refer to an author in passing, then place the parenthesis immediately after his or her name, again inside any adjacent punctuation:

```
Most authorities, including Zinsser (46) and Strunk
and White (6), emphasize that unity is one of the
bases of effective writing.
```

When you use a block quotation, place the parenthesis *one* letter space after the final period:

```
You learn to write by writing. It is a
truism worn thin by repetition, but it is
still true. . . . The only way to learn to
write is to force yourself to produce a
certain number of words on a regular
basis. (Zinsser 45)
```

The question often arises of what to do with several references occurring in quick succession. Must every clause or sentence contain a parenthesis? Not necessarily. By pulling together research material from the same page of a particular source, you can reference a whole paragraph of text using an author's name, accompanied by a page number in parentheses, in a sentence at the beginning of the paragraph and another page number in parentheses at the end. The reader understands that all the intervening material appears on the page referred to.

In a lengthy paragraph, you can remind your reader about your source by reintroducing the author's name or by using an appropriate pronoun, perhaps in conjunction with a quotation (for which, of course, you must provide a parenthetical page number). See "Summary" on pages 27-28 for an example.

If you refer to material from several different pages, then you must introduce the various page numbers in parentheses. And if you have referred to several different authorities, their names must appear appropriately, too. But often, as suggested above, you will be able to economize on the number of parentheses you use.

Sample References

- AUTHOR'S NAME AND TITLE IN TEXT
  (you referred to entire work so no page number, no parenthesis)

  ```
  William Zinsser's On Writing Well provides a wealth
  of good advice about writing.
  ```

- AUTHOR'S NAME IN TEXT WITH PAGE NUMBER IN PARENTHESIS
  (you did not refer to another work by same author)

  ```
  As William Zinsser has said, "Unity is the anchor
  of good writing" (46).
  ```

  Note: for a first reference in your sentence, you should use an author's full name as given on the title page, e.g., William Zinsser. Subsequently, the last name alone will suffice, i.e., Zinsser.

- AUTHOR'S NAME IN TEXT WITH ABBREVIATED TITLE IN PARENTHESIS
  (you referred to another work by same author)

  ```
  As William Zinsser has said, "Unity is the anchor
  of good writing" (Writing 46).
  ```

- AUTHOR'S NAME NOT IN TEXT
  (so last name in parenthesis)

  ```
  The beginning writer should always be aware that
  "Unity is the anchor of good writing" (Zinsser 46).
  ```

- AUTHOR'S NAME AND ABBREVIATED TITLE IN PARENTHESIS
  (you referred to another work by the same author)

  ```
  The beginning writer should always be aware that
  ```

"Unity is the anchor of good writing" (Zinsser, *Writing* 46).

● TWO OR THREE AUTHORS CITED IN PARENTHESIS

The purely visual impact of writing deserves attention: "paragraphing calls for a good eye as well as a logical mind" (Strunk and White 12).

● MORE THAN THREE AUTHORS CITED IN TEXT

Lauer et al. discuss ten points that are important in the writing process (2-3).

Note: "et al." is an abbreviation for the Latin *et alii*, meaning "and others."

● MORE THAN THREE AUTHORS CITED IN PARENTHESIS

At least ten points are important in the writing process (Lauer et al. 2-3).

● REFERENCE TO AN INDIRECT SOURCE
(original author mentioned in text)

According to R. D. Laing, "true sanity" requires "the dissolution of the normal ego, that false self competently adjusted to our alienated social reality . . ." (qtd. in Roszak 50).

Note: you discovered the quotation from Laing in a work by Roszak, and you wish to use part of it. As shown here, you must acknowledge both authors. The phrase "qtd. in"—the abbreviation for "quoted in"—indicates that your reader can locate the complete Laing quotation by looking under "Roszak" in your works cited. Do not provide an entry under "Laing" unless he is your direct source elsewhere in the essay. If, however, you think the original source may be of special interest to your reader, document it in a content note (see page 14). If you had paraphrased Laing's idea instead of quoting him, the parenthesis would still contain "qtd. in."

● REFERENCE TO AN INDIRECT SOURCE
(original author not mentioned in text so included in parenthesis)

```
We are told that "true sanity" requires "the
dissolution of the normal ego, that false self
competently adjusted to our alienated social
reality . . ." (Laing, qtd. in Roszak 50).
```

● REFERENCE TO AN UNSIGNED ARTICLE

```
In the southern part of the Selkirk Mountains lie
"vast areas of both igneous rocks of Mesozoic age
and very complex metamorphics" ("Selkirk").
```

Note: whenever your source does not provide the author's name, use an abbreviated version of the title. Here "Selkirk" corresponds to the word under which the work is alphabetized in works cited. No page number appears because the article is alphabetized in an encyclopedia, making the reference easily traceable. If the article appears in a periodical or newspaper, provide a page number.

● REPEATED REFERENCE TO ONE OR TWO WORKS

When you quote and/or paraphrase from *one* source (a novel, essay, etc.), give a *full footnote for the first reference* (see "The Note Style of Documentation" beginning on page 81), using an arabic superscript number, both in your text and in the footnote. Add to this footnote a short sentence directing the reader to the text references:

```
1 F. Scott Fitzgerald, The Great Gatsby (New
York: Scribner's, 1925) 23. Subsequent page
references are also to this edition.
```

Thus your text will contain references showing page numbers only, as in the following example. No works cited page is necessary since all of the information your reader needs is present in the footnote.

```
Although Nick sees that Tom and Daisy are

responsible for much of Gatsby's tragedy, he seems

unable to censure them completely, realizing that

"what he [Tom] had done was, to him, entirely

justified . . ." (180).
```

If you refer repeatedly to only *two* sources, provide two footnote references. This situation may arise in essays that compare or contrast. Your reader must, however, know clearly from your text which source you are referring to; therefore, to avoid confusion, include an author's name or a title in your sentence, or an author's name in your parenthesis.

If you use more than two sources, follow the regular conventions for text references, and provide a list of works cited.

References to Classic Literary Works

For some literary works, additional details may be required in the reference. For works of classic prose literature available in different editions, you should provide a chapter number, and a book number when relevant, in addition to the page number. Give the page number first; then, after a semicolon, give the extra detail(s) using abbreviations ("bk." for "book," "ch." for "chapter"):

```
In Tom Jones, Fielding humorously defends his right

to ransack the works of ancient authors without

either acknowledgment or scruple (474-75; bk. 12,

ch. 1).
```

Use arabic numerals instead of roman. In the above example, "XII" in the edition cited converts into "12." Note, too, that a comma goes between the book and chapter references.

For classic poems and verse plays, you should omit page numbers; instead, provide division numbers—i.e., the number of any book, canto, part, act, or scene—together with the line numbers:

```
                    Give me that man
That is not passion's slave, and I will wear him
In my heart's core, ay, in my heart of heart,
As I do thee. (Ham. 3.2. 67-70)
```

Note: in a parenthesis, though *not in the text*, the titles of famous works may be abbreviated: thus "Hamlet" becomes "Ham." In an essay exclusively on this play, however, where the source of the quotation is clear, it is not necessary to include the title in the parenthesis. Use periods to separate the numbers: in the above block quotation, "3" is the act number; "2" is the scene number; and "67-70" are the line numbers. Use arabic numerals. Do not signify lines by using the letters "l" or "ll."

References to the Bible or Other Sacred Texts

Unless you indicate otherwise, your reader will assume you are using the King James Version of the Bible, or the standard versions of other sacred works:

```
Few know that after the resurrection Jesus stayed
with his disciples for forty days, "speaking of the
things pertaining to the kingdom of God" (Acts 1:3).
```

Underlining, page numbers, and works cited entry are not required.

References to Nonprint Sources

When you acknowledge a nonprint source by a reference in your sentence, you eliminate the need for a parenthesis, since no page number is involved. You may include both a name (of an author, film director, radio or television artist, musician, etc.) and a title (of a play, film, radio or television program, record, audio-tape, CD-ROM, etc.), as in the following:

```
In Citizen Kane, Orson Welles created a virtual
encyclopedia of film technique.
```

Note: since the emphasis is on the director, his name should precede the title of the film in the list of works cited (see page 69).
Of course, a parenthesis *will* be required for the acknow-

ledgment of facts, information, and ideas from a source not introduced in your sentence:

Bizarre Books, soon to be published by Macmillan,
is a bizarre book listing and describing some of
the bizarrest works ever to appear on a hopeful
bookseller's shelves (As It Happens).

Works Cited

The works cited page should list *every* source you actually used in your text and for which you provided a text reference (do not fabricate a list of vaguely pertinent works you did not directly refer to). In the text-referencing system, this list is the sole provider of publishing (or broadcasting) details.

For book details, refer to the title page and the copyright page (the reverse of the title page), *not the cover*. Make a note of the title in full (including subtitle), the author(s), the city of publication, the year of publication, and the page number(s) for each reference. Other details should be recorded if present: editor(s); translator; author of foreword, afterword, preface, or introduction (only if named on the title page); edition and volume numbers; article, essay, story, and poem titles from collections; and whatever else may be necessary to enable your reader to track down the source you used. Save unnecessary return trips to the library by writing down *full* citations as you do your research.

Record equivalent details for nonprint sources. Refer to CD and cassette liner notes, introductory radio announcements, film, television, and CD-ROM credits, etc. For electronic mail, record the writer's name, the name of the person receiving the communication, and its date. For online bulletin board postings, record the author's name, the title of the document, the date it was posted, the name of the location where you found it, the date you found it, and the name of the source.

Remember that only some of these details go into your text references, while others are reserved for works cited.

Follow these rules when you prepare your list:

1. Centre the words `Works Cited` half an inch below the page number. The list always appears as the last page(s) of the essay.
2. Number each page of works cited, continuing the numbering of the text. The numbering on the sample works cited page (see page 54) follows MLA research-essay style with the page number accompanied by the writer's last name in a running headline. As an alternative, depending on your instructor's

52

wishes and the kind of essay you are writing, you may use the page number alone either centred or placed against the right margin half an inch from the top of the page.

3. For *every* source mentioned in your text, provide a corresponding entry in your works cited. The text reference and the entry in works cited must match.
4. Do not subdivide the list into categories unless asked to by your instructor.
5. Begin the first line of each entry at the left margin; indent subsequent lines of that entry by half an inch or five letter spaces.
6. Double space each entry, and double space between entries.
7. Do *not* number the entries.
8. List entries *alphabetically* by the *last name* of the first author (or director, commentator, creative artist, etc.) mentioned in the work's publishing or broadcasting information.
9. When no author is given, alphabetize the entry by the first word in the title. Disregard "A," "An," or "The," but leave the article in its usual place.
10. Capitalize the first and last words in the title (and subtitle, if any), and all the principal words. Do *not* capitalize articles, prepositions, coordinating conjunctions, or the "to" in infinitives. Separate a title and a subtitle with a colon.
11. Underline the title (and subtitle) of a separately published work; put quotation marks around article and essay titles.
12. Give the first city of publication listed on the title page or copyright page. To the name of an unfamiliar city, add an identifying detail: the abbreviated name of a US state, Canadian province, or English county, etc.
13. Use a shortened form of a publisher's name. Give only the first name, if more than one appears, and omit "Co.," "Inc.," etc. Use "Harper," rather than "Harper and Row Inc."
14. For books, give the year of publication recorded on the title page or on the copyright page after the symbol © (but do *not* include this symbol). Give the last *edition* date, but ignore reprint dates. If no date is given, write "n.d."
15. For daily and weekly publications, give the full date (day, month, year) of issue; for monthly publications give the month and year.

Sample Works Cited Page

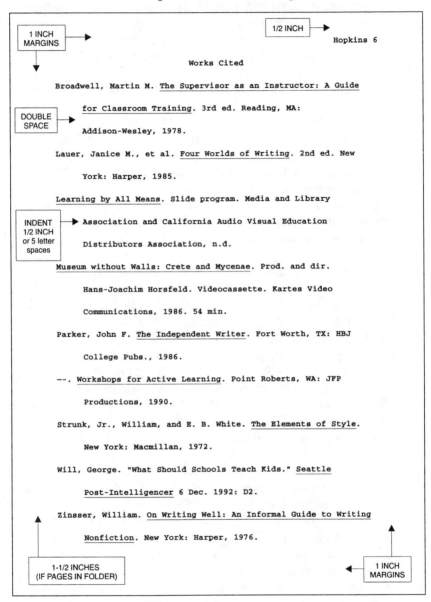

1 INCH MARGINS

1/2 INCH

Hopkins 6

Works Cited

Broadwell, Martin M. The Supervisor as an Instructor: A Guide

for Classroom Training. 3rd ed. Reading, MA:

DOUBLE SPACE

Addison-Wesley, 1978.

Lauer, Janice M., et al. Four Worlds of Writing. 2nd ed. New

York: Harper, 1985.

Learning by All Means. Slide program. Media and Library

INDENT 1/2 INCH or 5 letter spaces

Association and California Audio Visual Education

Distributors Association, n.d.

Museum without Walls: Crete and Mycenae. Prod. and dir.

Hans-Joachim Horsfeld. Videocassette. Kartes Video

Communications, 1986. 54 min.

Parker, John F. The Independent Writer. Fort Worth, TX: HBJ

College Pubs., 1986.

—-. Workshops for Active Learning. Point Roberts, WA: JFP

Productions, 1990.

Strunk, Jr., William, and E. B. White. The Elements of Style.

New York: Macmillan, 1972.

Will, George. "What Should Schools Teach Kids." Seattle

Post-Intelligencer 6 Dec. 1992: D2.

Zinsser, William. On Writing Well: An Informal Guide to Writing

Nonfiction. New York: Harper, 1976.

1-1/2 INCHES (IF PAGES IN FOLDER)

1 INCH MARGINS

16. For motion pictures, records, tapes, CD-ROMs, computer disk-ettes, and other media, give the year of release or issue. Give the full date for radio and television broadcasts, and interviews.
17. For most nonprint sources, state the medium of publication before the name of the manufacturer or distributor (see pages 68-73 for further details and examples).
18. Do *not* give page numbers unless you are citing an article in a journal, periodical, or newspaper, or an item in a collection (such as a short story or poem, etc.). Then give the page numbers of the *whole* article or item.
19. *Punctuate each entry carefully.* The sample works cited page (page 54) and the model entries that follow indicate the conventions for punctuating citations. Use a period followed by one letter space after each major division in a citation. Use a comma between an author's last and first names, and between the publisher's name and the year of publication, but use a colon after the city of publication.

Sample Citations

The list of works cited should employ the same conventions of indentation, order of items, use of underlining or quotation marks, punctuation, abbreviation, etc., illustrated below and in the sample page. Most of the types of sources you are likely to use are exemplified. *To cite a source, find a corresponding example from the entries that follow, and imitate the style.* If you can find no suitable model, consult pages 109-182 of the *MLA Handbook.*

Print Sources

● BOOK WITH ONE AUTHOR

Zinsser, William. <u>On Writing Well: An Informal Guide to Writing Nonfiction</u>. New York: Harper, 1976.

Note: leave one letter space after each major section of your citation, as shown throughout these examples.

● TWO OR MORE BOOKS BY THE SAME AUTHOR

Parker, John F. <u>The Independent Writer</u>. Fort Worth, TX: HBJ College Pubs., 1986.

—-. <u>Writing: Processed Product</u>. Evanston, IL: MacDougal, 1991.

Note: to indicate the repeated name, place three hyphens at the left margin followed by a period. If the name refers to an editor or translator, then place a comma after the hyphens followed by the appropriate abbreviation, e.g., —-, ed.

● BOOK WITH TWO OR THREE AUTHORS

Strunk, Jr., William, and E. B. White. <u>The Elements of Style</u>. New York: Macmillan, 1972.

Note: the first author's name is reversed, for the purpose of alphabetizing; subsequent names appear in their usual order.

● BOOK WITH MORE THAN THREE AUTHORS

Lauer, Janice M., et al. <u>Four Worlds of Writing</u>. 2nd

    ed. New York: Harper, 1985.

● BOOK WITH AUTHOR AND EDITOR
(you have quoted the author)

Freud, Sigmund. <u>A General Selection from the Works</u>

    <u>of Sigmund Freud</u>. Ed. John Rickman. Garden

    City, NY: Anchor-Doubleday, 1957.

Note: when citing the name of a publisher's special imprint—e.g., "Anchor"—give the imprint name first, followed by
a hyphen and the publisher's name.

● BOOK WITH AUTHOR AND EDITOR
(you have quoted the editor's preface)

Rickman, John, ed. Preface. <u>A General Selection from</u>

    <u>the Works of Sigmund Freud</u>. By Sigmund Freud.

    Garden City, NY: Anchor-Doubleday, 1957.

● BOOK IN TRANSLATION

Camus, Albert. <u>"The Myth of Sisyphus" and Other</u>

    <u>Essays</u>. Trans. Justin O'Brien. New York:

    Vintage, 1955.

● BOOK WITH INTRODUCTION BY ANOTHER AUTHOR
(you have quoted the introduction)

Corcoran, J. X. W. P. Introduction. <u>The Celts</u>. By

    Nora Chadwick. Harmondsworth, Middlesex:

    Penguin, 1970.

Note: Corcoran's name begins this citation because you quoted his introduction. Note, too, that "Introduction" appears in full with a period after it, and the word "By" precedes the name of the author. Use the same style when you quote from a foreword, afterword, or preface by another author.

● BOOK WITHOUT AUTHOR OR EDITOR

The National Geographic Atlas of the World. 5th ed.

Washington: Natl. Geog. Soc., 1981.

Note: this citation would be alphabetized by title under the letter "N" in the works cited without regard to "The."

● BOOK WITH CORPORATE AUTHOR
(committee, corporation, council, association, etc.)

Council on Economic Priorities. Star Wars: The

Economic Fallout. Cambridge, MA: Ballinger,

1987.

Note: "MA" is the abbreviation for Massachusetts. See the *MLA Handbook* for a comprehensive list of abbreviations of geographical names.

● BOOK WITH EDITION STATEMENT

Broadwell, Martin M. The Supervisor as an

Instructor: A Guide for Classroom Training. 3rd

ed. Reading, MA: Addison-Wesley, 1978.

● BOOK IN A SERIES

Parr, Richard T. A Bibliography of the Athapaskan

Languages. National Museum of Man. Mercury

Series, Ethnology Division 14. Ottawa: National

Museums of Canada, 1974.

Note: sometimes a publisher produces several volumes in the

same format, dealing with the same general area of research. Each book has its own title but belongs to a series. Include the name of the series and the number in the series if they are indicated, as in the example above. Underline the book title, but not the series name.

- REPUBLISHED BOOK

```
Collin, W. E. The White Savannahs. Introd. Germaine
    Warkentin. 1936. Toronto: U of Toronto P, 1975.
```

Note: this book was originally published in 1936. It went out of print and then was republished in 1975. The date of original publication is therefore given immediately before the publishing details for the republished edition. The abbreviation "U" stands for "University," and "P" stands for "Press."

- ANTHOLOGY OR COLLECTION
  (you have cited the editors)

```
Cone, Edward T., Joseph Frank, and Edmund Keeley,
    eds. The Legacy of R. P. Blackmur: Essays,
    Memoirs, Texts. New York: Ecco, 1987.
```

Note: the colon here, and in "Book With Edition Statement" above, introduces a subtitle. The subtitle often appears only on the title page, and is sometimes distinguished by a different typeface, but nonetheless you must include it in the full title in works cited.

- STORY IN AN ANTHOLOGY

```
Tyler, Anne. "Holding Things Together." We Are the
    Stories We Tell: The Best Short Stories by
    North American Women Since 1945. Ed. Wendy
    Martin. New York: Pantheon, 1990. 150-63.
```

Note: in this example, and in the one that follows, inclusive page numbers for the entire work cited appear at the end of the citation.

● ESSAY IN AN ANTHOLOGY

```
Illich, Ivan. "Outwitting Developed Nations." Toward
    a History of Needs. New York: Bantam, 1980.
    54-67.
```

● POEM IN A MULTIVOLUME ANTHOLOGY

```
Rossetti, Christina. "An Apple Gathering." 1861. The
    Norton Anthology of English Literature. Ed. M.
    H. Abrams et al. 4th ed. 2 vols. New York:
    Norton, 1979.
```

Note: if you wish, you may include the original date of publication, followed by a period, after the title. The number of the volume you referred to should accompany the page number(s) *in the parenthetical text reference* thus: (2: 1522-23).

● TWO OR MORE WORKS IN AN ANTHOLOGY

```
Gardner, Martin, ed. Great Essays in Science. New
    York: Washington Square, 1957.
```

```
Krutch, Joseph Wood. "The Colloid and the Crystal."
    Gardner 106-07.
```

```
Russell, Bertrand. "The Greatness of Albert
    Einstein." Gardner 398-402.
```

Note: to avoid repetition of publishing details when citing two or more different works in an anthology, list the anthology separately. For individual works referred to in your text, give the author's name, and the title, followed by the editor's last name and the page numbers for the entire work. Thus the name "Gardner" in the last two entries above provides a cross reference to the first entry, which contains the full publishing details.

● REVIEW OF A FILM, PLAY, BOOK, EXHIBITION, ETC.

```
Corliss, Richard.  "A Vampire With Heart."  Rev.  of

    Bram Stoker's Dracula, dir.  by Francis Ford

,   Coppola.  Time 30 Nov.  1992: 69.
```

Note: the abbreviation "dir." for "directed" indicates that a film review is being cited—"by" alone would signify a book review. Here Corliss is the reviewer, and "Rev. of" stands for "Review of." Observe that there is no punctuation between the magazine title and the date, but that a colon, followed by a letter space, goes between the year and the page number. For weekly magazines, the date replaces the volume number, and so is not enclosed in parentheses.

● ARTICLE IN A JOURNAL WITH A VOLUME NUMBER

```
Meier, Kathryn S.  "Tobacco Truths: The Impact of

    Role Models on Children's Attitudes Toward

    Smoking."  Health Education Quarterly 18.2

    (Summer 1991): 173-82.
```

Note: journals are scholarly publications appearing monthly, quarterly, or yearly. Magazines usually appear weekly or monthly and are more widely available, often at newsstands. The term "volume" refers to the collection of issues in an annual series.

If a journal begins each new issue with page 1, add a period and the issue number immediately after the volume number—in the example above, 18 is the volume number, and 2 is the issue number. Some libraries shelve journals by date rather than by number, so it is helpful to include the month (or season) and year in a parenthesis, as shown.

If a journal uses an issue number but not a volume number, include it as if it were the volume number.

If a journal has continuous pagination throughout the volume, i.e., does not begin each issue with page 1, give the volume number followed by the year of publication in a parenthesis, a colon, and the inclusive page numbers of the article you cited, as in the following example.

Rau, Santha Rama. "Benares: India's City of Light."
    National Geographic 169 (1986): 215-51.

● ARTICLE IN A WEEKLY OR MONTHLY MAGAZINE

"Exit Nixon." Time 19 Aug. 1974: 15-17.

Thomas, Lewis. "On the AIDS Problem." Discover May
    1983: 42+.

Note: the + sign in the above citation shows that the article begins on page 42 but is then interrupted by intervening material. For frequently published magazines, indicate the issue by date alone; omit volume and issue numbers.

● ARTICLE IN A NEWSPAPER (no author's name given)

"Those Were the Days." Vancouver Sun 10 Sept. 1980:
    D1.

Note: many newspapers paginate by section. In this case provide both section and page, without a space between. When a newspaper is paginated continuously, give the page number(s) alone.

● ARTICLE IN A NEWSPAPER (author's name given)

Clarke, Jack. "Learning the Lessons of War." The
    Province 7 March 1991: 41.

● ARTICLE IN A REFERENCE WORK
(no author's name given)

"San Bernardino Mountains." Encyclopedia Americana.
    1991 ed.

Note: because encyclopedias usually arrange articles alphabetically throughout, volume and page numbers are omitted. If the work is well known, specify only the edition, if stated, and the year of publication. For less well known reference works, give full publishing details.

```
"(Adeline) Virginia Woolf." Introduction. Twentieth-
     Century Literary Criticism. Vol. 5. 1981.
     505-06.
```

Note: here you begin with the title of the entire section on Woolf. You include "Introduction" because you referred to it and not the excerpts that follow it—no author is given. Because the series alphabetizes within each volume and not throughout, you give the volume number. You also include the page numbers for the introduction because it is only part of the section on Woolf.

- ● ARTICLE IN A REFERENCE WORK (author's name given)

```
Hills, Theo L. "Great Lakes." The World Book
     Encyclopedia. 1980 ed.
```

Note: if given, the author's name usually appears at the end of the article. Sometimes articles are signed with initials identified elsewhere in the work.

- ● ARTICLE REPRINTED IN A REFERENCE WORK (author's name given)

```
Thomas, Clara. "The Wild Garden and the Manawaka
     World." Modern Fiction Studies 22 (Autumn
     1976): 401-12. Excerpted under "Laurence,
     (Jean) Margaret" in Contemporary Literary
     Criticism. Vol. 13. 1980. 342-44.
```

Note: you referred to excerpts from Clara Thomas's previously published article. You give the original source first, and then the source you used after the words "Excerpted under." You use the word "Excerpt" because only parts of the original article are reprinted in your source, and "under" because "Laurence, (Jean) Margaret" is the alphabetized title under which the excerpts appear. If the whole article was reprinted, you would use

"Rpt." for "Reprinted" instead of "Excerpted." You include page numbers since your source is only part of the section on Laurence.

● YEARBOOK, ANNUAL

The Europa Year Book 1985: A World Survey. Vol. 1.
London: Europa, 1985.

● CONFERENCE PROCEEDINGS

Second National Forum on Handgun Control:
Proceedings. 7-9 Jan. 1976. Washington: United
States Conference of Mayors, 1976.

● ANNUAL REPORT

International Joint Commission. Annual Report on
Great Lakes Water Quality. Windsor, ON, 1978.

Great Britain. Colonial Office. Annual Report on the
Social and Economic Progress of the People of
Hong Kong. London, 1938.

● SPECIAL REPORT

City of Vancouver Task Force on Atmospheric Change.
Clouds of Change: Final Report. Vancouver, 1990.

● PAMPHLET

Acid Rain. Society for Promoting Environmental
Conservation (SPEC), n.d.

Note: sometimes pamphlets omit essential details, as here. No author is given or date of publication, hence the abbreviation "n.d." for "no date." But as far as possible, cite a pamphlet as if it were a book.

● RESERVE ARTICLE

Roberts, James D. Catholics, Divorce and Remarriage.
Photocopy of text of a lecture to the
conference of the Assn. of Separated and
Divorced Catholics, Toronto, 19 Sept. 1986.
Revised 1989. Placed on reserve at Langara
College Library, Vancouver.

Note: items placed on reserve are often published books or journal articles. In such cases, cite them in the normal manner, with full publishing details.

Government Sources

Citations for government-issued documents and publications usually begin with the jurisdiction, or government name, which stands in place of an author's name. This may be followed by the relevant department, agency, office, committee, or other subdivision of the government structure.

● PARLIAMENTARY DEBATE

Canada. Parliament. House of Commons. Debates.
Official Report. 33rd Parliament. 2nd session.
Vol. 14, 6 July - 17 Aug., 1988. Ottawa:
Queen's Printer, 1990.

British Columbia. Legislative Assembly. Debates.
Official Report. (Hansard.) 34th Parliament.
3rd session. Vol 15, 6 July - 20 July, 1989.
Victoria: Queen's Printer, 1990.

● COMMITTEE REPORT

Canada. Parliament. House of Commons. Standing
   Committee on National Health and Welfare.
   Report on AIDS in Canada. Ottawa: Queen's
   Printer, 1986.

United States. Congress. House. Select Committee on
   Aging. Subcommittee on Health and Long-term
   Care. Elder Abuse: A National Disgrace. A
   report by Rep. Claude Pepper, subcommittee
   chair. 99th Cong., 1st sess. Committee print.
   Washington: GPO, 1985.

Note: "Queen's Printer" is the publisher-of-record for many federal goverment documents. In the US, the United States Government Printing Office (GPO), publishes the *Congressional Record* and thousands of federal government documents.

● STATUTE

Canada. Competition Act, R.S.C. 1985, c. C-34, as
   am. by R.S.C. 1985, c. 19 (2nd Supp.), s. 19
   [formerly the Combines Investigation Act].

Note: the citation for an act, or a section of an act, is presumed to include the amendments to it. You would list amendments only if you had specifically referred to them. "R.S.C." stands for "Revised Statues of Canada"; C-34 is the chapter number; "am." is the abbreviation for "amended," "c" is for "chapter." and "s." is for "section."

British Columbia. Education Excellence Appropriation
   Repeal Act, S.B.C. 1988, c. 10.

Note: "S.B.C." stands for "Statutes of British Columbia."

● BILL

Bill C-9, <u>An Act to Facilitate Combatting the</u>
<u>Laundering of Proceeds of Crime</u>. 34th
Parliament. 3rd session, 1991. (Second Reading,
20 June 1991.)

Note: the "C" for "Commons"—House of—in the bill number
indicates the jurisdiction. Bills originating in the Senate bear an
"S." Since bills are numbered from 1 in each parliament, include
the parliament number, the session, the sessional year(s), the
reading, and the reading date. Do the same for provincial
bills—see below.

Bill 90, <u>Property Rights Act</u>. 34th Parliament. 4th
session, B.C., 1991. (Second Reading, 21 March
1991.)

Note: for provincial bills, begin with the bill number and include
the jurisdiction following the session number.

● BY-LAW

City of Vancouver. <u>Downtown Office Development Plan</u>.
(Adopted by By-Law No. 4912, 4 Nov. 1975.)

● GOVERNMENT PUBLICATION (author or editor given)

United States. Dept. of State. <u>The United States and</u>
<u>Russia: The Beginning of Relations, 1765-1815</u>.
Ed. Nina N. Bashkina, et al. Washington: GPO,
1980.

Note: use "By" instead of "Ed." when an author's name is given.
Or, you may begin the citation with the name of the author or
editor. Better still, cross reference the item by author or editor
name, as below:

Bashkina, Nina N., et al., eds. 1980. See US Dept.

of State. 1980.

● ROYAL COMMISSION REPORT

Canada. Royal Commission on Bilingualism and

Biculturalism. Final Report. 6 vols. Ottawa:

Queen's Printer, 1967-1970.

Nonprint Sources

For audiocassettes, audio tapes (reel to reel), videocassettes, videodiscs, long-playing records (abbreviated as "LP"), slide programs, film strips, microforms, computer diskettes, CD-ROMs, online materials, electronic mail, and interviews, state the medium (before the name of the manufacturer or distributor where applicable). Naming the medium is not required for compact discs, motion pictures, radio and television programs, and works of art.

When constructing your works cited page, imitate the forms of appropriate entries selected from the following list.

● TELEVISION PROGRAM

Cat On a Hot Tin Roof. By Tennessee Williams. Dir.

Jack Hofiss. American Playhouse. PBS. KCTS/9,

Seattle. 31 July 1985.

Note: the series title, American Playhouse, appears after the program reference, and is not underlined or put in quotation marks. PBS is the network, and KCTS/9 is the broadcast station.

● RADIO PROGRAM

As It Happens. CBC Radio. CBU, Vancouver. 29 May

1996.

Note: CBC Radio is the network; CBU is the local broadcast station.

- MOTION PICTURE

> Welles, Orson, dir. <u>Citizen Kane</u>. With Welles and
>   Joseph Cotten. RKO, 1941.

Note: Welles and Cotten are identified as principal actors. Other individuals may be mentioned when relevant to your text, e.g., producer, screenwriter, film score composer, etc. If you have emphasized the film rather than the director in your text, the title should appear first with the director's name following.

- AUDIO RECORDING (compact disc, LP, audiocassette, audiotape)

> Sainte-Marie, Buffy. "Eagle Man/Changing Woman." <u>Up</u>
>   <u>Where We Belong</u>. EMI Music Canada, E235059,
>   1996.

Note: the disc number, or record album (LP) number, or tape number appears after the name of the recording company.

> Ellington, Duke. "A Tone Parallel to Harlem (The
>   Harlem Suite)." 1951. <u>Uptown</u>. Audiocassette.
>   CBS, WCT40836, n.d.

Note: the above audiocassette is a re-release of previously recorded material. The cassette's liner notes indicate 1951 as the original recording date. No date is given for the issue of this cassette, hence "n.d."

- VIDEO RECORDING

> <u>The Human Experiment</u>. Ethics in America Series 9.
>   Videocassette. Santa Barbara: Intellimation,
>   1989.

Note: treat a videodisc in exactly the same way but substitute the term "videodisc" for "videocassette."

● SLIDE PROGRAM

Learning by All Means. Slide program. Media and
    Library Association and California Audio Visual
    Education Distributors Association, n.d.

Note: "n.d." indicates no date is given for the issue of this slide program. If a date is given, include it.

● FILMSTRIP

Michelangelo: The Sistine Chapel. Filmstrip. Life
    Filmstrips, 1950.

● WORK OF ART

Van Gogh, Vincent. Starry Night. Museum of Modern
    Art, New York.

Note: underline the title of a sculpture, a painting, or any other 'published' work of art and name the institution that houses the work.

● MICROFORM (microfilm, microfiche, microprint, etc.)

Richardson, Penelope L. "Issues in Television-
    centered Instruction." Proceedings of the
    Annual Meeting of the American Educational
    Research Association, Los Angeles, April 1981.
    ERIC Document Reproduction Services ED20521
    (1981).

Note: give details for the original source of the work cited; then give the name (underlined) of the microform source you actually used, followed by the volume number and the year (in parentheses). Put a colon instead of a period after the date and add fiche and grid numbers if they will assist the reader to locate the relevant material.

● CD-ROM

"Abolitionist Movement." Compton's Interactive
Encyclopedia. CD-ROM. N.p.: Compton's New
Media, Inc. 1994.

Note: in this example, an encyclopedia article, no author is given
and "N.p." indicates that no place or city of publication is given.
If known, the author's name would precede the title in the
normal fashion.

● ELECTRONIC DOCUMENT
(accessed through a computer service)

Elkin, Stanley. "American Fiction and its Reach."
Harper's Magazine. Mar. 1992: 34+. Magazine
Database Plus. Online. CompuServe. 18 Dec. 1995.

Note: if you cite an electronic version of previously published
print materials, your citation should begin with the original
version details, following the style used for printed sources. In
addition, include the name of the database (underlined); the
medium ("Online"); the name of the computer service used to
access the database ("CompuServe" in the example above); and
the date you accessed the material.

● ELECTRONIC DOCUMENT
(accessed through a computer network)

Beauregard, Erving E. "Robert Hanna—Theoretical
Terrorist in Abolitionism and Antimasonry."
Online Modern History Review. (Dec. 1992):
n. pag. Online. Internet. 16 Dec. 1995.
Available: gopher://vifa1.freenet.victoria.bc.
ca:70/00/archives/history/reviewed/beauregard.

Note: the above-cited article has not appeared in print. The
notation "n. pag." means no pagination is given. If the number
of online "pages" or paragraphs is given, include them (e.g. "10

pp." or "36 pars.") Include the name of the network used to access the material, and your access date. Because managers of electronic documents can move, copy, and revise them easily, you must give the location where *you* found a document and *your* date of access. End your citation with the electronic address of the material, introduced with "Available:".

Davis, L. J. "Medscam: A Mother Jones

Investigation." <u>Mother Jones Magazine</u>.

Mar.-Apr. 1995. Online. MoJo Wire. Internet.

1 Dec. 1995. Available: http://www.mojones.com/

mother_jones/MA95/davis.html.

Note: complete details of the print version may not be provided online. The magazine article cited above is from a "full text archive" but there is no reference to the print-version page numbers. Include as many details as are available, including the name of the archive or repository of the electronic text ("MoJo Wire" in the example above). Be sure to include your access date and the network location of the material.

● ELECTRONIC MAIL

Volkmer, Jon. "Regarding goldfish." E-mail to

Raymond Bendall. 12 June 1995.

Note: use the message's "Subject" heading as a title if the message is not titled in any other way. If no title or subject is present, the citation is shortened to:

Volkmer, Jon. E-mail to Raymond Bendall. 12 June

1995.

● INTERVIEW

Prince, Linda. Personal interview. 2 Aug. 1991.

Note: personal interviews should be distinguished from telephone interviews. In general, an interview has weight only when you are citing an authority—someone with informed opinions. Indicate his or her credentials in your text:

```
College librarian Linda Prince said that. . . .
```

See the *MLA Handbook* for how to document interviews from magazines, radio, or television.

● SPEECH or LECTURE

```
Carr, Shirley. "The Trade Union Outlook on Serious
     Concerns of the 1990s and Beyond." Empire Club
     of Canada. Royal York Hotel, Toronto. 15 March
     1990.
```

Note: if there is no title, indicate the type of oral presentation given, e.g., speech, lecture, reading, etc. Do not underline this designation or put it in quotation marks.

The APA Style of Documentation

The influential American Psychological Association (APA) advocates a somewhat different system, often referred to as the author-date system, both for indicating sources of paraphrases, summaries, and quotations in the text of an essay and for listing references at the end. APA style is designed for writers who intend to publish their papers. The advice that follows is therefore adapted to meet the needs of college students. With minor variations, the social sciences (Psychology, Anthropology, and Sociology) and some physical sciences (e.g., Biology) employ the APA conventions outlined here.

Below is a sample page from a long article that was accepted for publication. It illustrates several major features of APA style including page format, a variety of typical references for paraphrase and summary, and the use of direct quotations. The writer used APA software that will paginate, print running heads, and help build a proper list of works cited. Student papers may not require page headings. Consult your instructor.

Page Format

1. For your title page you may use a layout similar to that in the sample on page 11. Although it does not correspond in all respects to APA publication style, it is suitable for college-level essays. APA convention requires that titles appear in upper- and lower-case letters and not in all capitals (check the rules for capitalization on page 53).
2. A running head appears flush right in the upper right corner of every page, including the title page, a half inch from the top edge. The heading includes the essay title, if brief, or is a shortened form of a long title, followed by five letter spaces, and then the page number.
3. The text begins one inch from the top of the page.

Sample APA Style Text Page

In terms of the clinical/reminiscence domain there has been an emerging emphasis on the distinction between "historical truth" and "narrative truth" (Bruner, 1986; Spence, 1984). The former connotes a static reservoir of directly (although not necessarily easily) retrievable and unimpeachable "facts"; the latter explicitly acknowledges the reconstructive and dynamic nature of memory recall and is more concerned with its verisimilitude than with documentable accuracy. Within the parameters of narrative truth, clinicians and clients jointly facilitate the retrieval and elucidation of memories which form a life portrait supported by current self-structures (e.g., Webster & Young, 1988). This is a dynamic process leading to narrative revisions, defined by Bonanno (1990) as "the re-evaluation or re-experiencing of the past in the context of a new conceptual framework" (p. 176).

In terms of autobiographical memories, McAdams (1989) demonstrated that personality factors (i.e., themes of intimacy and power) were strongly associated with autobiographical memories of "peak experiences." Specifically, themes of intimacy or power were higher in peak experience protocols of subjects who had correspondingly high themes on prior projective

Text References

1. Parenthetical references do not contain titles.
2. When you use paraphrase or summary and refer to the author in your sentence, the parenthesis contains only the date of publication.
3. When you use paraphrase or summary without mentioning the author in the sentence, your reference should include the author(s), followed by a comma, and the date.
4. Use an ampersand (&) instead of "and" for two authors in a parenthetical reference: (Webster & Young, 1988).
5. When you quote an author whose name is in your sentence, provide the date in parentheses immediately after the name, and a page reference (using "p." or "pp.") directly after the quotation and before the sentence period. (See the last sentence of the first paragraph of the sample page.)
6. When you quote without indicating the author in your text, the reference after the quotation is as follows:

   " . . . narrative revisions" (Webster, 1991, p. 65).

7. If two or more works by the same author were published in the same year, distinguish between them in references by coding each with lower-case "a," "b," "c," etc., in order of their appearance in your list of works cited:

   Bonanno (1988b) proposes that the true . . .

8. If more than one source has contributed to the content of a summary or paraphrase, arrange them in alphabetical order by author; include the dates, and use a semicolon to separate them:

   (Bruner, 1986; Spence, 1984)

Using Notes in APA Style

Content or informational notes use the same numbering convention as for MLA note style (see page 14), but the notes are double-spaced under the heading Footnotes on a separate page following the references page. Indent the first line of each note five spaces from the left margin.

Bibliographical Citations

Though a list of works cited and a list of references in APA style are identical in many respects, there are important differences. As with any style, the APA is strict about the order and form of the parts of an entry.

1. Begin a fresh page (continuing the pagination of the text) by centring the word References one inch from the top.
2. Begin each entry at the left margin. Subsequent lines are indented five or seven letter spaces.
3. Double-space throughout the list.
4. For more than one author, all names appear in reverse order (not just the first); give all surnames in full, others in initials only; use "&" instead of "and" before the last name. Note: in a text reference, if there are more than six authors mention only the first, using "et al." for the others.
5. List two or more works by the same author(s) in chronological order (earliest publication first), spelling out the author's full name in each entry.
6. Place a period after each major part of an entry.
7. Following the name(s) of the author(s), place the date in a parenthesis—hence the term "author-date" system.
8. If you have used two or more works published in the same year by the same author or co-authors, code the dates in succession with "a" then "b" then "c," and so on.
9. Next comes the title of the book or article. For a book, underline title (and subtitle), and capitalize only the first word of title (and subtitle); for an article, do not use quotation marks or underlining, and capitalize as for a book title, including all proper names.
10. The city of publication and the name of the publisher, linked by a colon, precede the final period (e.g., second model entry).
11. The name of a journal, using upper- and lower-case letters, is underlined. A comma separates it from the volume number (in arabic numerals, without "vol."), which is also underlined (e.g., last entry).
12. If volumes of a journal are numbered continuously, provide inclusive page numbers for the article, without "pp." (e.g., last entry).
13. If each issue in a volume is numbered separately, include the

issue number in a parenthesis following the volume number (e.g., first entry).

14. If the article is from an edited collection or anthology (not a periodical), the word "In" introduces the name of the editor(s), followed by "ed." or "eds." plus a comma, and then the book title (underlined). Inclusive page numbers follow directly in a parenthesis (no punctuation precedes), with "pp." to indicate "pages" (e.g., third entry).

Sample APA Style References

Reminiscence   87

References

Bonanno, G. A. (1990). Remembering and psychotherapy.

Psychotherapy, 27(2), 175-186.

Bruner, J. (1986). Actual minds, possible worlds. Cambridge, MA:

Harvard University Press.

McAdams, D. P. (1989). The development of a narrative identity.

In D. M. Buss, & N. Cantor (Eds.), Personality psychology:

Recent trends and emerging directions (pp. 124-132). New

York: Springer-Verlag.

Spence, D. P. (1984). Narrative truth and historical truth.

New York: Norton.

Webster, J. D., & Young, R. A. (1988). Process variables of the

life review: Counselling implications. International

Journal of Aging and Human Development, 26, 315-323.

Documenting Research in Sociology

Essays in Sociology follow the basic APA guidelines given above, with a few differences:

TEXT REFERENCES
1. No comma after the author(s).
2. Parenthetical references usually include page numbers.
3. No "p." or "pp." in parentheses. Typical references:

```
(Giddens 1987, 15); (Giddens 1979c, 37-38)
```

WORKS CITED
1. The list may be labeled either "References" or "Works Cited."
2. The position of the year of publication may be in either MLA or APA style.

Consult the section on APA style above for all other matters of form. For further guidance, ask your instructor for models or imitate the conventions used in currently published articles in the field. Ultimately, instructors are almost universally agreed that the greatest virtue in your documentation style ought to be *consistency*.

Documenting Research in Biology

Biology essays use APA conventions, with some exceptions:

TEXT REFERENCES
1. For two authors, use "and" not "&" in the parenthesis:

```
(Smith and Jones, 1991).
```

2. Place a comma after the author(s).
3. Quotations are generally not used.
4. If you must quote or indicate a specific page from a book, the page number follows the date and a colon, without "p." or "pp.":

```
The Indole test was performed to isolate Salmonella
from Edwardsiella (Barnett, 1988: 380); a negative
result confirmed Salmonella.
```

5. As shown above, references usually appear inside your sentences, as close as possible to the material you have used.
6. In order to show that several consecutive pieces of information in your paragraph have the same source, place the reference at the end, after the sentence period:

> . . . and confirmed that <u>Salmonella</u> usually produces hydrogen sulfide. (Sneath, 1984: 415)

Note: in both references and citations, Latin names for species are underlined.

WORKS CITED

1. The list of works cited is headed with `Literature Cited` or `References`.
2. Include names of all authors, spelling out the last names only and using initials for first and middle names.
3. Following the author(s) comes the year of publication, standing alone without parentheses.
4. Write out the complete title of an article, without quotation marks and capitalizing only the first word:

> Singer, S. J., and G. Nicholson. 1972. Fluid mosaic model of the structure of cell membranes. <u>Science</u> 175: 720.

5. Abbreviate complex journal names but not one-word names.
6. Following the volume number (without "vol.") of a journal, a colon precedes the inclusive page numbers given in full:

> <u>Marine Biol</u>. 85: 157-166.

7. For book titles, indicate volume number, if any (use "Vol."), publishing information, and pages consulted (use "pp."). The publisher precedes the city with a comma between them.

> Laskin, A. I., and H. A. Lechevalier, eds. 1973. <u>CRC Handbook of Systematic Microbiology</u>. Vol. 2. Williams and Williams, Baltimore, MD., pp. 118-124.

The Note Style of Documentation

Although parenthetical text-referencing systems of documentation are widely used, in some courses you may still be expected to use numbered footnotes or endnotes to acknowledge sources. Many books and articles employ this traditional method, so you should familiarize yourself with its basic conventions, in any case.

Ask your instructor whether you should use footnotes or endnotes. In general, the more notes you have, the more practical it is to gather them together as endnotes at the end of the text.

Placement of Notes and Note Numbers

In the note system, quotations, paraphrases, and other uses of source material are numbered consecutively from [1] throughout the text with arabic superscripts (numbers that go a half space above the line). They are then acknowledged in correspondingly numbered notes that appear either at the foot of the text pages, or on a separate page (or pages) under the heading Notes immediately following the end of the text.

Good word processing programs will help you create footnotes and endnotes, handling the placing of superscript numbers and the spacing of lines. If you use such a program, obviously you must accept its conventions.

The guidelines below follow both MLA style and Turabian.

1. Place a superscript number in your text immediately following any phrase, clause, or sentence that contains quoted, paraphrased, or summarized material.
2. Place the number outside any final punctuation (except a dash).
3. Leave a letter space after the number but not in front of it.
4. Do not punctuate the number in any way.
5. Match this text number to a footnote number (superscript) at the bottom of the page, or to an endnote number (superscript) on a separate page at the end of the text.
6. Write the note after the appropriate note number.

See the following sample essay page showing the placement of numbers in the text and the corresponding footnotes.

Content of First Notes

For the first reference to a book give full details. Include in the note the author's full name as given on the title page, the title (including subtitle, if any), the name of an editor or translator (if any), the volume and edition numbers (if any), the city of publication, the publisher's name, the date of publication, and the page number of the reference. Provide corresponding information for other works—see the sample entries that follow.

The convention used to be that if a bibliographical detail—most commonly the author's name—appeared in the text, it was not repeated in the note. However, Turabian sensibly rules that the author's name must appear in the note, regardless of whether it is a first note or a subsequent note (except when ibid. is used).

Note Layout

1. Begin footnotes four line spaces below the text.
2. Indent the first line of a note five letter spaces from the left margin; begin subsequent lines at the margin.
3. Double space footnotes and endnotes. Double space between entries.
4. Leave one letter space between the superscript number and the beginning of the note.
5. First and last names of authors appear in the normal order.
6. Place a comma between the author's name and the title of the work, and between the publisher's name and the date of publication. Put parentheses around the city of publication, the publisher, and the year of publication. Place a colon followed by one letter space between the city of publication and the publisher's name. Be sure to put a period at the end of the entry. Leave only one letter space between major parts of the note.
7. Do *not* use the abbreviations "p.", "pp." or "pg." before the page number.

Subsequent Notes

The first time you acknowledge a source, provide full details, as indicated above. For all subsequent references to the same source, use one of the abbreviated forms of the note described below.

Sample Note Style Text Page

frequently in the past."[12] On February 26, however, the Cunard liner Laconia was sunk.[13] The sinking of the Algonquin followed on March 12; and then, on March 19, word arrived of the sinking of three American ships within a space of twenty-four hours.[14] As other options disappeared, the President realized that "his choice lay between acquiescing in the German submarine campaign or calling upon Congress for a declaration of war."[15] He chose the latter course.

Charles Seymour disputes the view that President Wilson's decision was unduly influenced by interest groups acting for the allies, saying,

> There is no scrap of valid evidence supporting this thesis, and all that is available directly controverts it. At the beginning of the war Wilson declared and believed that it could not touch us, that if we kept clean neutral hands we were fulfilling our duty and preserving our security. He was speedily disabused.[16]

[12] Ernest R. May, ed., The Coming of War, 1917, The Berkeley Series in American History (Chicago: Rand McNally, 1963), 41.

[13] Ibid.

[14] Charles Seymour, "America Enters the War," in Intervention, 1917: Why America Fought, ed. Warren I. Cohen, Problems in American Civilization Series (Boston: Heath, 1966), 56.

[15] May, 48.

[16] Seymour, 57.

SUCCESSIVE REFERENCES

When references to a particular source follow one another immediately, with no other reference intervening, use "ibid." (an abbreviation of the Latin *ibidem* meaning "in the same place") instead of repeating the whole note.

Add only those details that are different in the new note—usually a page number. Note 13 on the sample page is a second reference to the same page in the same work by May, noted immediately above. If this note referred to another page in May's work, page 43 for example, it would read, `Ibid., 43.`

SEPARATED REFERENCES

When references to a particular source are separated by other references, use the author's last name alone in the subsequent note, together with the page number (whether different or not). Thus in note 16 on the sample page, the name "Seymour" refers the reader to note 14 and the work entitled "America Enters the War."

If you had referred to two works by Seymour, then you would distinguish between them in the subsequent note by including an abbreviated form of the title:

`16 Seymour, "America," 57.`

Note Terms and Abbreviations

The traditional footnote method employed Latin abbreviations to indicate subsequent references. The *MLA Handbook* and Turabian both recommend against their continued use, preferring the simple repetition of an author's last name, plus a page number. But since they appear in already published works, you should understand their meaning:

loc. cit. (*loco citato*)
means "in the place (or passage) cited," i.e., in the same passage referred to in a nearby note. It is preceded by an author's name, in the note or in the text, but is not followed by a page number since the passage has already been identified in the previous note.

op. cit. (*opere citato*)
means "in the work cited." It is used when referring to a passage

on a different page of a work noted nearby. Again it is preceded by an author's name in note or text, but this time a new page number appears.

Three Latin terms are, however, still widely used in the note system of documentation. One has been mentioned above, "ibid.," which is used to refer to the work mentioned in the immediately preceding note. Another is "passim," meaning "here and there." Use it in a note together with page numbers or a chapter number to indicate that the material referred to is scattered throughout a particular section of the text: e.g., "60-95 passim" or "chap. 3 passim." The abbreviation "et al." (*et alii*), meaning "and others," may be used when you refer in a note to a work with more than three authors.

Works Cited

A list of works cited may not be needed, especially if you have already listed your notes as endnotes at the end of the text. Ask your instructor. If a works cited list is necessary, follow the guidelines set out on pages 52-55.

Sample Notes

● BOOK WITH ONE AUTHOR

[1] W. J. Reader, Life in Victorian England (London: Batsford, 1964), 42.

Note: punctuate notes with commas except in front of a parenthesis.

● BOOK WITH MORE THAN THREE AUTHORS

[2] Yuko Shibata, et al., The Forgotten History of the Japanese Canadians, vol. 1 (Vancouver: New Sun Books, 1977), 10.

● BOOK WITH EDITOR

³ Veronica Strong-Boag, ed., <u>A Woman with a Purpose: The Diaries of Elizabeth Smith, 1872-1884</u> (Toronto: U of Toronto P, 1980), 102.

● ESSAY IN AN ANTHOLOGY

⁴ L. J. Evenden, and I. D. Anderson, "The Presence of a Past Community: Tashme, British Columbia," <u>Peoples of the Living Land</u>, ed. Julian V. Minghi (Vancouver: Tantalus Books, 1972), 63.

● ARTICLE IN A JOURNAL WITH A VOLUME NUMBER

⁵ Chad Gaffield, "Children, Schooling, and Family Reproduction in Nineteenth Century Ontario," <u>Canadian Historical Review</u> 72 (June 1991), 157-91.

Note: in this journal, pagination is continuous within each volume, so the issue number is omitted. If each issue of a journal is paginated separately, put a period after the volume number and add the issue number, e.g., 72.2. Add the date of issue in parentheses after the volume number. The page numbers at the end refer to the whole article.

● ARTICLE IN A WEEKLY OR MONTHLY MAGAZINE

⁶ Roger Rosenblatt, "What Really Mattered? Not Just Great Events But Underlying Causes," <u>Time</u>, 5 Oct. 1983, 22-25.

⁷ Kishu Singh, and Dilip Bobb, "Perishtroika, Mon Amour," <u>New Internationalist</u>, Sept. 1990, 20.

Note: indicate the issue by date alone; omit volume and issue numbers.

- ARTICLE IN A NEWSPAPER (no author's name given)

    [8] "West Begins Recognizing Baltic States," The Globe and Mail, 26 Aug. 1991, A1.

- ARTICLE IN AN ENCYCLOPEDIA (author's name given)

    [9] Donald MacGillivray Nicol, "Byzantine Empire," Encyclopaedia Britannica: Macropaedia, 1974 ed.

Note: this article is signed at the end with initials only. To find the name of the author, look up "D.M.N." in the volume entitled *Propaedia: Guide to the Britannica*. To find the article, look up the alphabetized title. Because articles are alphabetized throughout the work, volume and page numbers are omitted.

- PARLIAMENTARY DEBATE

    [10] Canada, House of Commons, Debates, Official Report, 32nd Parliament, 1st session, vol. 5 (Ottawa: Queen's Printer, 1980): 5537.

Index

Abbreviations, 22
Alphabetizing, works cited, 53
American Psychological Association
    See APA
Ampersand, in APA style, 76
Annual report, 64
Anthology, 59
    component part of, 59, 60, 86
    multiple works in, 60
    part of multivolume, 60
APA style, 74
    ampersand in, 76
    citations, 77
    page format, 74
    sample list of references, 78
    text references, 76
    use of notes, 76
Apostrophe, 23
Appendix, 14
Art, works of, 70
Audio recording, 69
Audiocassette, 69
Audiotape, 69
Author-date system
    See APA style
Author-date citations, 77
Author's name
    in reference, 46
    in text, 46
    unknown, 48

Bible, references to, 50
Bill, government, 67
Biology, style for, 79
Block quotations
    See also Quotations
    colon before, 32
    ellipsis in, 34
    indentation of, 32
    parenthetical reference for, 33, 45

spacing of, 32
use of, 32
Book
    with author and editor, 57
    without author or editor, 58
    with corporate author, 58
    with edition statement, 58
    with editor, 86
    introduction by another author, 57
    with multiple authors, 56, 85
    multiple works by one author, 56
    republished, 59
    in series, 58
    with single author, 56, 85
    in translation, 57
Book report, 8
Brackets, 35
By-law, 67

Capitalization of title, 53
CD-ROM, 71
Citations
    See also Works cited
    APA style, 77
    in biology, 80
    defined, 1
    page numbers in, 55
    publication details in, 53
    punctuation in, 55
    in sociology, 79
Collection
    See Anthology
Colon
    before subtitle, 10
    before quotations, 31, 32
Comma
    before quotations, 31
Committee report, 66
Compact disc (CD), 69
Conference proceedings, 64

Content notes, 14
Corrections, 16
Critique, 8

Dates
    in citations, 53
    in text, 22
Discriminatory language, 24
Drama, quoting, 41

Electronic document
    accessed through a computer
        network, 71
    accessed through a computer
        service, 71
Electronic mail, 72
Ellipsis, in quotations, 34
Encyclopedia article, 62, 87
Endnotes
    See Notes
Epigraph, 12
Essay, development of, 13
Et al., 47, 85
Expository essay, 4

Film
    See Motion picture
Filmstrip, 70
Folders, 17
Fonts, 20
Footnotes
    See Notes

Government publications, 65

Hyphenation, 20

Ibid., 84, 85
Illustrations, 13
Indentation
    of block quotations, 32
    of paragraphs, 13
    in works cited, 53
Indirect sources, reference to, 47
Interview, 72

Italics
    See also Underlining
    and word processors, 21
    in quotations, 40

Journal article, 61, 86

Lecture, 73
Literary insight essay, 6
Literary works, reference to, 49
Loc. cit., 84
Long-playing record (LP), 69

Magazine article, 62, 86
Margins, 17, 20
Microforms, 70
Motion picture, 69

Newspaper article, 62, 87
Nonprint sources, 50, 55, 68
Notes
    in APA style, 76
    content, 14
    first reference, 48, 82
    format of, 82, 83
    numbering of, 81
    placement of, 81
    repeated references, 48, 82
    sample, 85
    separated references, 84
    terms and abbreviations, 84
Numbers, spelled out, 22
Numerals, 22

Omissions, from quotations, 34
Op. cit., 84

Page format
    in APA style, 74
    of text, 16
    works cited, 52, 54
Page numbers
    in citations, 55
    in parenthetical references, 43
Pagination, of essay, 17

Pamphlet, 64
Paper, for essays, 16
Paraphrasing, 25
Parenthesis, to subordinate
quotation, 31
Parenthetical references
See also References
author-date system, 77
with block quotation, 45
effects of, 43
forms of, 42
with multiple authors, 47
page number in, 43
placement of, 44
with single author, 46
with title abbreviated, 46
Parliamentary debate, 65, 87
Passim, 85
Personal experience essay, 4
Plagiarism, 24
Plays, line numbers with, 49
Poetry
line numbers with, 49
quoting, 38
Proofreader's symbols, 19
Publication details, in citations, 53
Punctuation
See Comma, etc.

Quotation marks
around title, 53
for brief quotations, 30
for part within whole, 22
single, 36, 40
for title within title, 12
within quotation, 36
Quotations
See also Block quotations
altering with brackets, 35
closing punctuation, 37
colon before, 31
comma before, 31
defined, 28
drama, 41
ellipsis in, 34

errors in, 36
incorporated in text, 30
italics in, 40
omissions from, 34
poetry, 38
references for, 30
subordination of, 31
underlining added to, 40
underlining in, 40
use of, 29, 33
within a quotation, 36

Radio program, 68
Reference work, article in, 62
References
See also Parentheti cal references
APA style, 78
author unknown, 48
in biology, 79
content for printed sources, 42
defined, 1
incorporated in text, 43
to indirect source, 47
to literary works, 49
for quotations, 30
repeated, 45, 48
to sacred texts, 50
samples, 46
in sociology, 79
use of, 42
Research essay, 5
Research, primary, 5
Research report, 7
Research, secondary, 5
Reserve article, 65
Review, 61
Roman numerals, converting, 49
Royal Commission, 68

Sacred texts, references to, 50
Sic, 36
Slides, 70
Sociology, style for, 79

Spacing
    of block quotations, 32
    of text, 13, 17
    of works cited, 53
Special report, 64
Speech, 73
Spell-checking software, 21
Statute, 66
Style, defined, 1
Subheadings, 13
Subtitle, 10, 59
Summarizing, 27
Summary, 8

Table of contents, 12
Tables, 13
Technical essay, 7
Television program, 68
Title (of work)
    abbreviated in parenthesis, 46, 50
    capitalizing, 53
    effective, 10
    quotation marks around, 53

underlining, 12, 22, 53
    within a title, 12
Title page, 9
Typing, 16

Underlining (or italicizing), 12, 21,
    22, 40, 53

Videotape, 69

Word processors, 16, 20
    and back-ups, 21
    font selection, 20
    hyphenating with, 20
Works cited
    alphabetizing, 53
    defined, 15, 52
    indentation, 53
    page format, 52, 54
    spacing, 53

Yearbook, 64